Anonymous

Hymns Recommended for Use in the Reformed Episcopal Church

Anonymous

Hymns Recommended for Use in the Reformed Episcopal Church

ISBN/EAN: 9783337297022

Printed in Europe, USA, Canada, Australia, Japan

Cover: Foto ©Lupo / pixelio.de

More available books at **www.hansebooks.com**

HYMNS

RECOMMENDED FOR USE

IN THE

REFORMED EPISCOPAL CHURCH.

PHILADELPHIA:
CHARLES W. QUICK,
OFFICE OF THE LEIGHTON PUBLICATIONS,
1225 SANSOM STREET.
1874.

HYMNS.

ADVENT.

HYMN 1. C. M.

Hark! the glad sound, the Saviour comes,
   The Saviour promised long;
Let every heart prepare a throne,
   And every voice a song.

2.

On him the Spirit, largely pour'd,
   Exerts his sacred fire;
Wisdom and might, and zeal and love,
   His holy breast inspire.

3.

He comes, the prisoners to release,
   In Satan's bondage held;
The gates of brass before him burst,
   The iron fetters yield.

4.

He comes, from thickest films of vice
   To clear the mental ray;
And on the eyes oppress'd with night
   To pour celestial day.

5.

He comes, the broken heart to bind,
  The bleeding soul to cure,
And with the treasures of his grace,
  To enrich the humble poor.

6.

Our glad Hosannas, Prince of Peace,
  Thy welcome shall proclaim;
And heaven's eternal arches ring
  With thy beloved Name.

HYMN 2. 8s, 7s.

Hail! thou long expected Jesus,
  Born to set thy people free;
From our fears and sins release us;
  Let us find our rest in thee.

2.

Israel's strength and consolation,
  Hope of all the earth thou art;
Long desired of every nation,
  Joy of every waiting heart.

3.

Born thy people to deliver,
  Born a child, yet God our King,
Born to reign in us for ever,
  Now thy gracious kingdom bring.

4.

By thine own eternal Spirit,
  Rule in all our hearts alone:

ADVENT.

By thine all-sufficient merit,
  Raise us to thy glorious throne.

HYMN 3. C. M.

JOY to the world! the Lord is come:
  Let earth receive her King:
Let every heart prepare him room,
  And heaven and nature sing.

2.

Joy to the earth! the Saviour reigns:
  Let men their songs employ;
While fields, and floods, rocks, hills, and plains,
  Repeat the sounding joy.

3.

Let the whole earth his love proclaim,
  With all her different tongues,
And spread the honours of his name
  In melody and songs.

4.

No more let sins and sorrows grow,
  Nor thorns infest the ground;
He comes to make his blessings flow,
  Far as the curse is found.

5.

He rules the world with truth and grace,
  And makes the nations prove
The glories of his righteousness,
  And wonders of his love.

HYMN 4. 8s, 7s, 4s.

Lo, he comes, with clouds descending,
  Once for favored sinners slain;
Thousand thousand saints attending
  Swell the triumph of his train;
    Hallelujah!
  God appears on earth to reign.

2.

Every eye shall now behold him,
  Robed in dreadful majesty;
Those who set at nought and sold him,
  Pierced, and nailed him to the tree,
    Deeply wailing,
  Shall the true Messiah see.

3.

Every island, sea, and mountain,
  Heaven and earth, shall flee away:
All who hate him must, confounded,
  Hear the trump proclaim the day;
    Come to judgment,
  Come to judgment, come away.

4.

Now redemption, long expected,
  See in solemn pomp appear:
All his saints, by men rejected,
  Now shall meet him in the air:
    Hallelujah!
  See the day of God appear.

CHRISTMAS.

5.

Yea, Amen; let all adore thee,
 High on thine eternal throne:
Saviour, take the power and glory;
 Claim the kingdom for thine own.
 O come quickly!
Hallelujah! Come, Lord, come!

CHRISTMAS.

HYMN 5. 7s.

HARK! the herald angels sing,
 Glory to the new-born King;
Peace on earth, and mercy mild;
God and sinners reconciled.

2.

Joyful all ye nations rise,
Join the triumph of the skies;
With th' angelic host proclaim,
Christ is born in Bethlehem!

3.

Christ, by highest heaven adored,
Christ, the everlasting Lord,
In th' appointed time has come;
Every heart now make him room.

4.

Veil'd in flesh, the Godhead see:
Hail th' incarnate Deity,

Pleased, as man, with man to dwell;
Jesus, now Emmanuel.

5.

Risen with healing in his wings,
Light and life to all he brings;
Hail the Sun of Righteousness!
Hail the heaven-born Prince of Peace!

HYMN 6. II. M.

Chorus.

SHOUT the glad tidings, exultingly sing;
Jerusalem triumphs, Messiah is King!

1.

Sion, the marvellous story be telling,
    The Son of the Highest, how lowly his birth!
The brightest archangel in glory excelling,
    He stoops to redeem thee, he reigns upon earth!

Chorus.

Shout the glad tidings, exultingly sing;
Jerusalem triumphs, Messiah is King!

2.

Tell how he cometh; from nation to nation,
    The heart-cheering news let the earth echo round;

CHRISTMAS.

How freely he giveth his finished salvation,
  How his people with joy everlasting are crowned.

Chorus.
Shout the glad tidings, exultingly sing;
Jerusalem triumphs, Messiah is King!

3.
Mortals, your homage be gratefully bringing,
  And sweet let the gladsome hosanna arise;
Ye angels, the full Hallelujah be singing;
  One chorus resound through the earth and the skies:

Chorus.
Shout the glad tidings, exultingly sing;
Jerusalem triumphs, Messiah is King!

HYMN 7. 8s, 7s, 4s.

ANGELS, from the realms of glory,
  Wing your flight o'er all the earth;
Ye, who sang creation's story,
  Now proclaim Messiah's birth;
    Come and worship,
Worship Christ, the new-born King.

2.
Shepherds, in the field abiding,
  Watching o'er your flocks by night,

God with man is now residing;
  Yonder shines the infant light:
    Come and worship,
    Worship Christ, the new-born King.

3.

Sages, leave your contemplations,
  Brighter visions beam afar:
See the great Desire of nations;
  Ye have seen his natal star:
    Come and worship,
    Worship Christ, the new-born King.

4.

Saints, before the Saviour bending,
  Waiting long in hope and fear,
Suddenly, the Lord, descending,
  In mid-heaven shall appear:
    Come and worship,
    Worship Christ, the new-born King.

HYMN 8. C. M.

WHILE shepherds watched their flocks
    by night,
  All seated on the ground,
The angel of the Lord came down,
  And glory shone around.

2.

"Fear not," said he, for mighty dread
  Had seized their troubled mind;
"Glad tidings of great joy I bring
  To you, and all mankind.

3.

"To you, in David's town, this day
  Is born, of David's line,
The Saviour, who is Christ the Lord;
  And this shall be the sign.

4.

"The heavenly babe you there shall find,
  To human view displayed,
All meanly wrapt in swathing bands,
  And in a manger laid."

5.

Thus spake the seraph; and forthwith
  Appeared a shining throng
Of angels, praising God, and thus
  Address'd their joyful song:

6.

"All glory be to God on high,
  And to the earth be peace;
Good will henceforth, from heaven to men,
  Begin, and never cease."

HYMN 9. 7s.

JESUS! Name of wondrous love!
Name all other names above!
Unto which must every knee
Bow in deep humility.

2.

Jesus! Name of priceless worth
To the fallen sons of earth,

For the promise that it gave—
"Jesus shall his people save."

3.

Jesus! Name of mercy mild,
Given to the holy Child,
When the cup of human woe
First he tasted here below.

4.

Jesus! only name that's given
Under all the mighty heaven,
Whereby man, to sin enslaved,
Bursts his fetters and is saved.

5.

Jesus! Name of wondrous love!
Human Name of God above;
Pleading only this, we flee,
Helpless, O our God, to thee.

HYMN 10. C. M.

CALM on the listening ear of night
  Came heaven's melodious strains,
Where wild Judea stretches far
  Her silver-mantled plains.

2.

Celestial choirs from courts above
  Shed sacred glories there;
And angels, with their sparkling lyres,
  Make music on the air.

3.

The answering hills of Palestine
  Send back the glad reply;
And greet, from all their holy heights,
  The Day-Spring from on high.

4.

O'er the blue depths of Galilee
  There comes a holier calm,
And Sharon waves, in solemn praise,
  Her silent groves of palm.

5.

"Glory to God!" the sounding skies
  Loud with their anthems ring,
"Peace to the earth, good-will to men,
  From heaven's eternal King!"

6.

Light on thy hills, Jerusalem!
  The Saviour now is born!
And bright on Bethlehem's joyous plains
  Breaks the first Christmas morn.

HYMN 11. 8s, 7s.

HARK! what mean those holy voices
  Sweetly sounding through the skies?
Lo! the angelic host rejoices,
  Heavenly hallelujahs rise.

2.

Listen to the wondrous story
  Which they chant in hymns of joy—

"Glory in the highest, glory!
   Glory be to God most high!

3.

"Peace on earth, good-will from heaven,
   Reaching far as man is found;
Souls redeemed and sins forgiven,
   Loud our golden harps shall sound.

4.

"Christ is born; the great Anointed!
   Heaven and earth his praises sing!
O receive whom God appointed
   For your Prophet, Priest and King!

5.

"Hasten, mortals, to adore him;
   Learn his name to magnify,
Till in heaven ye sing before him.
   Glory be to God most high!"

HYMN 12. 10s.

RISE, crown'd with light, imperial Salem, rise;
Exalt thy towering head and lift thine eyes;
See heaven its sparkling portals wide display,
And break upon thee in a flood of day.

2.

See a long race thy spacious courts adorn,
See future sons, and daughters yet unborn,

In crowding ranks on every side arise,
Demanding life, impatient for the skies.

3.

See barbarous nations at thy gates attend,
Walk in thy light, and in thy temple bend:
See thy bright altars throng'd with prostrate kings,
While every land its joyous tribute brings.

4.

The seas shall waste, the skies to smoke decay,
Rocks fall to dust, and mountains melt away;
But fix'd his word, his saving power remains;
Thy realm shall last, thy own Messiah reigns.

HYMN 13. 7s, 6s.

HAIL to the Lord's Anointed,
   Great David's greater Son!
Hail, in the time appointed,
   His reign on earth begun!
He comes to break oppression,
   To set the captive free,
To take away transgression,
   And rule in equity.

2.

He comes with succor speedy,
   To those who suffer wrong,

To help the poor and needy,
   And bid the weak be strong;
To give them songs for sighing,
   Their darkness turn to light,
Whose souls, condemn'd and dying,
   Were precious in his sight.

3.

He shall descend like showers
   Upon the fruitful earth;
And love and joy, like flowers,
   Spring in his path to birth:
Before him, on the mountains,
   Shall peace, the herald, go;
And righteousness, in fountains,
   From hill to valley flow.

4.

To him shall prayer unceasing,
   And daily praise ascend;
His kingdom still increasing,
   A kingdom without end:
The tide of time shall never
   His covenant remove;
His name shall stand for ever:
   That Name to us is Love.

EPIPHANY.

HYMN 14. 11s, 10s.

BRIGHTEST and best of the sons of the morning,
   Dawn on our darkness, and lend us thine aid;

EPIPHANY.

Star of the East, the horizon adorning,
   Guide where our infant Redeemer is laid.

2.

Cold on his cradle the dew-drops are shining,
   Low lies his head with the beasts of the stall;
Angels adore him in slumber reclining,
   Maker and Monarch and Saviour of all.

3.

Say, shall we yield him, in costly devotion,
   Odors of Eden, and offerings divine,
Gems of the mountain, and pearls of the ocean, -
   Myrrh from the forest, and gold from the mine?

4.

Vainly we offer each ample oblation,
   Vainly with gifts would his favor secure;
Richer by far is the heart's adoration,
   Dearer to God are the prayers of the poor.

5.

Brightest and best of the sons of the morning,
   Dawn on our darkness, and lend us thine aid:

Star of the East, the horizon adorning,
  Guide where our infant Redeemer is laid.

HYMN 15. S. M.

How beauteous are their feet
  Who stand on Sion's hill;
Who bring salvation on their tongues,
  And words of peace reveal!

2.

How charming is their voice:
  How sweet their tidings are!
"Sion, behold thy Saviour-King,
  He reigns and triumphs here."

3.

How happy are our ears
  That hear this joyful sound,
Which kings and prophets waited for,
  And sought, but never found!

4.

How blessèd are our eyes
  That see this heavenly light!
Prophets and kings desired it long,
  But died without the sight.

5.

The watchmen join their voice,
  And tuneful notes employ;
Jerusalem breaks forth in songs,
  And deserts learn the joy.

EPIPHANY.

6.

The Lord makes bare his arm
  Through all the earth abroad:
Let every nation now behold
  Their Saviour and their God.

HYMN 16.   7s.

WATCHMAN! tell us of the night,
  What its signs of promise are;
Traveller! o'er yon mountain's height,
  See that glory-beaming star.
Watchman! does its beauteous ray
  Aught of joy or hope foretell?
Traveller! yes; it brings the day,
  Promised day of Israel.

2.

Watchman! tell us of the night:
  Higher yet that star ascends.
Traveller! blessedness and light,
  Peace and truth, its course portends.
Watchman! will its beams alone
  Gild the spot that gave them birth?
Traveller! ages are its own;
  See, it bursts o'er all the earth.

3.

Watchman! tell us of the night.
  For the morning seems to dawn.
Traveller! darkness takes its flight;
  Doubt and terror are withdrawn.
Watchman! let thy wanderings cease;
  Hie thee to thy quiet home.

Traveller! lo! the Prince of Peace,
  Lo! the Son of God is come.

HYMN 17. L. M.

WHEN, marshal'd on the nightly plain,
  The glittering host bestud the sky,
One star alone of all the train
  Can fix the sinner's wandering eye.

2.

Hark! hark! to God the chorus breaks,
  From every host, from every gem;
But one alone the Saviour speaks;
  It is the Star of Bethlehem.

3.

It is my guide, my light, my all,
  It bids my dark forebodings cease;
And through the storm and danger's thrall,
  It leads me to the port of peace.

4.

Then, safely moor'd, my perils o'er,
  I'll sing, first in night's diadem,
For ever and for evermore,
  The Star, the Star of Bethlehem!

LENT.

HYMN 18. 7s.

SAVIOUR, when in dust, to thee,
Low we bow th' adoring knee;
When, repentant, to the skies,
Scarce we lift our streaming eyes;

LENT.

O, by all thy pain and woe,
Suffer'd once for man below,
Bending from thy throne on high,
Hear our solemn litany.

2.

By thy birth and early years,
By thy human griefs and fears,
By thy fasting and distress
In the lonely wilderness,
By thy victory in the hour
Of the subtle tempter's power;
Jesus, look with pitying eye;
Hear our solemn litany.

3.

By thy conflict with despair,
By thine agony in prayer,
By the purple robe of scorn,
By thy wounds, thy crown of thorn,
By thy cross, thy pangs and cries.
By thy perfect sacrifice;
Jesus, look with pitying eye;
Hear our solemn litany.

4.

By the bright'ning, heavens above,
By thy finished work of love,
By thy triumph o'er the grave,
By thy power from death to save;
Mighty God, ascended Lord,
To thy throne in heaven restored,
Prince and Saviour, hear our cry,
Hear our solemn litany.

HYMN 19. C. M.

HOW oft, alas! this wretched heart
  Has wandered from the Lord:
How oft my roving thoughts depart,
  Forgetful of his word!

2.

Yet sovereign mercy calls, "Return;"
  Dear Lord, and may I come?
My vile ingratitude I mourn;
  O, take the wanderer home.

3.

And canst thou, wilt thou yet forgive,
  And bid my crimes remove?
And shall a pardon'd rebel live
  To speak thy wondrous love?

4.

Almighty grace, thy healing power,
  How glorious, how divine!
That can to life and bliss restore
  So vile a heart as mine.

5.

Thy pardoning love, so free, so sweet,
  Dear Saviour, I adore:
O, keep me at thy sacred feet,
  And let me rove no more.

HYMN 20. L. M.

O THAT my load of sin were gone,
  O that I could at last submit
At Jesus' feet to lay it down,
  To lay my soul at Jesus' feet.

LENT.

2.
Rest for my soul I long to find;
  Saviour of all, if mine thou art,
Give me thy meek and lowly mind,
  And stamp thine image on my heart.
3.
Break off the yoke of inbred sin,
  And fully set my spirit free;
I cannot rest till pure within,
  Till I am wholly lost in thee.
4.
Fain would I learn of thee, my God;
  Thy light and easy burden prove,
The cross, all stain'd with hallow'd blood,
  The labor of thy dying love.
5.
I would, but thou must give the power,
  My heart from every sin release;
Bring near, bring near the joyful hour,
  And fill me with thy perfect peace.

HYMN 21. L. M.

O THOU to whose all-searching sight
  The darkness shineth as the light,
Search, prove my heart; it pants for thee,
O burst these bonds, and set it free.

2.
Wash out its stains, refine its dross,
Nail my affections to the cross;
Hallow each thought; let all within
Be clean, as thou, my Lord, art clean.

3.

If in this darksome wild I stray,
Be thou my light, be thou my way;
No foes, no violence I fear,
No harm, while thou, my God, art near.

4.

When rising floods my soul o'erflow,
When sinks my heart in waves of woe,
Jesus, thy timely aid impart,
And raise my head, and cheer my heart.

5.

Saviour, where'er thy steps I see,
Dauntless, untired, I follow thee;
O let thy hand support me still,
And lead me to thy holy hill.

6.

If rough and thorny be the way,
My strength proportion to my day,
Till toil, and grief, and pain shall cease,
Where all is calm, and joy, and peace.

HYMN 22. L. M.

MY God, permit me not to be
A stranger to myself and thee:
Amidst a thousand thoughts I rove,
Forgetful of my highest love.

2.

Why should my passions mix with earth,
And thus debase my heavenly birth?
Why should I cleave to things below,
And all my purest joys forego?

3.

Call me away from flesh and sense;
Thy grace, O Lord, can draw me thence:
I would obey the voice divine,
And all inferior joys resign.

HYMN 23. H. M.

NEARER, my God, to thee,
   Nearer to thee,
E'en though it be a cross
   That raiseth me;
Still all my song shall be,
Nearer, my God, to thee,
   Nearer to thee.

2.

Though like the wanderer,
   The sun gone down,
Darkness be over me,
   My rest a stone;
Yet in my dreams I'd be
Nearer, my God, to thee,
   Nearer to thee.

3.

There let my way appear
   Steps unto heaven;
All that thou sendest me
   In mercy given;
Angels to beckon me
Nearer, my God, to thee,
   Nearer to thee.

HYMNS.

4.

Then with my waking thoughts
　Bright with thy praise,
Out of my stony griefs
　Altars I'll raise;
So by my woes to be
Nearer, my God, to thee,
　Nearer to thee.

5.

Or if on joyful wing,
　Cleaving the sky,
Sun, moon, and stars forgot,
　Upward I fly,
Still all my song shall be
Nearer, my God, to thee,
　Nearer to thee.

HYMN 24.　C. M.

O GRACIOUS God, in whom I live,
　My feeble efforts aid;
Help me to watch, and pray, and strive,
　Though trembling and afraid.

2.

Increase my faith, increase my hope,
　When foes and fears prevail;
And bear my fainting spirit up,
　Or soon my strength will fail.

3.

Whene'er temptations fright my heart,
　And lure my feet aside,

My God, thy powerful aid impart,
　My guardian and my guide.

4.

O keep me in thy heavenly way,
　And bid the tempter flee;
And let me never, never stray
　From happiness and thee.

PASSION WEEK AND GOOD FRIDAY.

HYMN 25. L. M.

WHEN I survey the wondrous cross,
　On which the Prince of Glory died,
My richest gain I count but loss,
　And pour contempt on all my pride.

2.

Forbid it, Lord, that I should boast,
　Save in the cross of Christ my God:
All the vain things that charm me most,
　I sacrifice them to thy blood.

3.

See! from his head, his hands, his feet,
　Sorrow and love flow mingled down:
Did e'er such love and sorrow meet?
　Or thorns compose a Saviour's crown?

4.

Were the whole realm of nature mine,
　That were a tribute far too small;
Love so amazing, so divine,
　Demands my life, my soul, my all.

HYMN 26. C. M.

BEHOLD the Saviour of mankind
  Nail'd to the shameful tree;
How vast the love that him inclined
  To bleed and die for me!

2.

Hark, how he groans! while nature shakes,
  And earth's strong pillars bend;
The temple's vail in sunder breaks,
  The solid marbles rend.

3.

'Tis done! the precious ransom's paid;
  "Receive my soul!" he cries;
See where he bows his sacred head!
  He bows his head and dies.

4.

But soon he'll break death's envious chain,
  And in full glory shine;
O Lamb of God, was ever pain,
  Was ever love like thine!

HYMN 27. 8s, 7s.

WHO is this that comes from Edom,
  All his raiment stained with blood,
To the captive speaking freedom,
  Bringing and bestowing good;
Glorious in the garb he wears,
Glorious in the spoil he bears?

2.

'Tis the Saviour, now victorious,
　Travelling onward in his might;
'Tis the Saviour; O how glorious,
　To his people, is the sight!
Satan conquered, and the grave,
Jesus now is strong to save.

3.

Why that blood his raiment staining?
　'Tis the blood of many slain;
Of his foes there's none remaining,
　None, the contest to maintain:
Fallen they are, no more to rise;
All their glory prostrate lies.

4.

Mighty Victor, reign for ever;
　Wear the crown so dearly won;
Never shall thy people, never,
　Cease to sing what thou hast done;
Thou hast fought thy people's foes;
Thou hast healed thy people's woes.

HYMN 28.　8s, 7s.

HAIL, thou once despisèd Jesus!
　Hail, thou Galilean King,
Thou didst suffer to release us,
　Thou didst free salvation bring:
Hail, thou agonizing Saviour,
　Bearer of our sin and shame;
By thy merit we find favor,
　Life is given through thy name.

2.

Paschal Lamb by God appointed,
   All our sins were on thee laid;
By Almighty love anointed,
   Thou hast full atonement made.
Every sin may be forgiven,
   Through the virtue of thy blood;
Opened is the gate of heaven,
   Peace is made for man with God.

3.

Jesus, hail! enthroned in glory,
   There for ever to abide,
All the heavenly host adore thee,
   Seated at thy Father's side:
There for sinners thou art pleading;
   "Spare them yet another year;"
Thou for saints art interceding,
   Till in glory they appear.

4.

Worship, honor, power, and blessing,
   Thou art worthy to receive:
Loudest praises, without ceasing,
   Meet it is for us to give.
Help, ye bright angelic spirits;
   Bring your sweetest noblest lays;
Help to sing our Saviour's merits,
   Help to chant Immanuel's praise.

HYMN 29.   8s, 7s.

SWEET the moments, rich in blessing,
   Which before the cross I spend;

Life, and health, and peace possessing,
  From the sinner's dying Friend.

2.

Here I'll sit, for ever viewing
  Mercy's streams, in streams of blood;
Precious drops, my soul bedewing,
  Plead, and claim my peace with God.

3.

Truly blessèd is the station,
  Low before his cross to lie;
While I see divine compassion
  Beaming in his languid eye.

4.

Lord, in ceaseless contemplation
  Fix my thankful heart on thee,
Till I taste thy full salvation,
  And thine unveil'd glory see.

HYMN 30. C. M.

FOR ever here my rest shall be,
  Close to thy bleeding side;
This all my hope and all my plea,
  "For me the Saviour died."

2.

My dying Saviour and my God,
  Fountain for guilt and sin!
Sprinkle me ever with thy blood,
  And cleanse and keep me clean.

3.

Wash me, and make me thus thine own;
  Wash me, and mine thou art;
Wash me, but not my feet alone—
  My hands, my head, my heart.

4.

Th' atonement of thy blood apply,
  Till faith to sight improve;
Till hope in full fruition die,
  And all my soul is love.

HYMN 31. L. M.

'TIS finished: so the Saviour cried,
  And meekly bow'd his head and died:
'Tis finished: yes, the work is done,
The battle fought, the victory won.

2.

'Tis finished: all that heaven decreed,
And all the ancient prophets said,
Is now fulfill'd, as long designed,
In me, the Saviour of mankind.

3.

'Tis finished: Aaron now no more
Must stain his robes with purple gore:
The sacred vail is rent in twain,
And Jewish rites no more remain.

4.

'Tis finished: this my dying groan
Shall sins of every kind atone:

EASTER.

Millions shall be redeem'd from death,
By this, my last expiring breath.

5.
'Tis finished: heaven is reconciled,
And all the powers of darkness spoiled:
Peace, love, and happiness, again
Return and dwell with sinful men.

6.
'Tis finished: let the joyful sound
Be heard through all the nations round:
'Tis finished: let the echo fly
Through heaven and hell, through earth
  and sky.

EASTER.

HYMN 32. 7s.

CHRIST the Lord is risen to-day!
  Sons of men and angels say:
Raise your joys and triumphs high,
Sing, ye heavens, and earth reply.

2.
Love's redeeming work is done,
Fought the fight, the victory won:
Jesus' agony is o'er,
Darkness vails the earth no more.

3.
Vain the stone, the watch, the seal,
Christ hath burst the gates of hell:
Death in vain forbids him rise,
Christ hath opened Paradise.

4.
Lives again our glorious King;
Where, O Death, is now thy sting?
Once he died, our souls to save;
Where's thy victory, O Grave?

5.
Soar we now where Christ hath led,
Following our exalted Head;
Made like him, like him we rise:
Ours the cross, the grave, the skies.

HYMN 33. L. M.

OUR Lord is risen from the dead,
  Our Jesus is gone up on high;
The powers of hell are captive led,
  Dragged to the portals of the sky.

2.
There his triumphal chariot waits,
  And angels chant the solemn lay:
"Lift up your heads, ye heavenly gates,
  Ye everlasting doors give way."

3.
Loose all your bars of massy light,
  And wide unfold th' ethereal scene;
He claims those mansions as his right,
  Receive the King of glory in.

4.
Who is the King of glory?—who?
  The Lord, that all his foes o'ercame;
The world, sin, death, and hell o'erthrew,
  And Jesus is the Conqueror's name.

EASTER.

5.

Lo! his triumphal chariot waits,
  And angels chant the solemn lay:
"Lift up your heads, ye heavenly gates,
  Ye everlasting doors give way."

6.

Who is the King of glory?—who?
  The Lord, of glorious power possessed;
The King of saints and angels too,
  God over all for ever blessed.

HYMN 34. L. M.

YE faithful souls who Jesus know,
  If risen indeed with him ye are,
Superior to the joys below,
  His resurrection's power declare:

2.

Your faith by holy tempers prove,
  By actions show your sins forgiven,
And seek the glorious things above,
  And follow Christ, your Head, to heaven.

3.

There your exalted Saviour see,
  Seated at God's right hand again,
In all his Father's majesty,
  In everlasting power to reign.

ASCENSION.

HYMN 35. P. M.

REJOICE, the Lord is King;
   Your God and King adore:
Ye saints, give thanks and sing,
   And triumph evermore.
Lift up the heart, lift up the voice,
Rejoice, again I say, rejoice.

2.

Jesus the Saviour reigns,
   The God of truth and love!
When he had washed our stains,
   He took his seat above.
Lift up the heart, lift up the voice,
Rejoice, again I say, rejoice.

3.

His kingdom cannot fail,
   He rules o'er earth and heaven;
The keys of death and hell
   Are to our Jesus given.
Lift up the heart, lift up the voice,
Rejoice, again I say, rejoice.

4.

He all his foes shall quell,
   Shall all our sins destroy,
And every bosom swell
   With pure seraphic joy:
Lift up the heart, lift up the voice,
Rejoice, again I say, rejoice.

WHIT-SUNDAY.

5.

Rejoice in glorious hope,
  Jesus the Judge shall come.
And take his servants up
  To their eternal home.
We soon shall hear th'archangel's voice,
The trump of God shall sound, Rejoice.

WHIT-SUNDAY.

HYMN 36. C. M.

COME, Holy Spirit, heavenly Dove,
  With all thy quickening powers;
Kindle a flame of sacred love
  In these cold hearts of ours.

2.

See how we grovel here below,
  Fond of these earthly toys:
Our souls, how heavily they go,
  To reach eternal joys.

3.

In vain we tune our lifeless songs,
  In vain we strive to rise;
Hosannas languish on our tongues,
  And our devotion dies.

4.

Dear Lord, and shall we ever live
  At this poor dying rate?
Our love so faint, so cold to thee,
  And thine to us so great?

5.

Come, Holy Spirit, heavenly Dove,
  With all thy quickening powers;
Come, shed abroad a Saviour's love,
  And that shall kindle ours.

HYMN 37. C. M.

HE'S come, let every knee be bent,
  All hearts new joy resume;
Sing, ye redeemed, with one consent,
  "The Comforter is come."

2.

What greater gift, what greater love,
  Could God on man bestow?
Angels for this rejoice above,
  Let man rejoice below.

3.

Hail, blessed Spirit! may each soul
  Thy sacred influence feel;
Do thou each sinful thought control,
  And fix our wavering zeal.

4.

Thou to the conscience dost convey
  Those checks which we should know;
Thy motions point to us the way;
  Thou giv'st us strength to go.

HYMN 38. S. M.

COME, Holy Spirit, come:
  Let thy bright beams arise;

TRINITY SUNDAY.

Dispel the sorrow from our minds,
The darkness from our eyes.

2.
Revive our drooping faith,
Our doubts and fears remove,
And kindle in our breasts the flame
Of never-dying love.

3.
Convince us of our sin;
Then lead to Jesus' blood,
And to our wondering view reveal
The mercies of our God.

TRINITY SUNDAY.
HYMN 39. L. M.

O HOLY, holy, holy Lord,
Bright in thy deeds and in thy Name,
For ever be thy Name adored,
Thy glories let the world proclaim.

2.
O Jesus, Lamb once crucified
To take our load of sins away,
Thine be the hymn that rolls its tide
Along the realms of upper day.

3.
O Holy Spirit from above,
In streams of light and glory given,
Thou source of ecstacy and love,
Thy praises ring through earth and heaven.

4.

O God Triune, to thee we owe
  Our every thought, our every song;
And ever may thy praises flow
  From saint and seraph's burning tongue.

HYMN 40. L. M.

FATHER of all, whose love profound
  A ransom for our souls hath found,
Before thy throne we sinners bend;
To us thy pardoning love extend.

2.

Almighty Son, incarnate Word,
Our Prophet, Priest, Redeemer, Lord,
Before thy throne we sinners bend;
To us thy saving grace extend.

3.

Eternal Spirit, by whose breath
The soul is raised from sin and death,
Before thy throne we sinners bend;
To us thy quickening power extend.

4.

Jehovah! Father, Spirit, Son,
Mysterious Godhead, Three in One!
Before thy throne we sinners bend;
Grace, pardon, life, to us extend.

HYMN 41. 8s, 7s, 4s.

HOLY Father, great Creator,
  Source of mercy, love, and peace,

Look upon the Mediator,
  Clothe us with his righteousness;
    Heavenly Father,
  Through the Saviour hear and bless.

2.

Holy Jesus, Lord of glory,
  Whom angelic hosts proclaim,
While we hear thy wondrous story,
  Meet and worship in thy name,
    Dear Redeemer,
  In our hearts thy peace proclaim.

3.

Holy Spirit, Sanctifier,
  Come with unction from above,
Raise our hearts to raptures higher,
  Fill them with the Saviour's love!
    Source of comfort,
  Cheer us with the Saviour's love.

4.

God the Lord, through every nation
  Let thy wondrous mercies shine!
In the song of thy salvation
  Every tongue and race combine!
    Great Jehovah,
  Form our hearts and make them thine.

THANKSGIVING DAY.

HYMN 42.   7s.

PRAISE to God, immortal praise,
  For the love that crowns our days;

Bounteous source of every joy,
Let thy praise our tongues employ:
All to thee, our God, we owe,
Source whence all our blessings flow.

2.

All the blessings of the fields,
All the stores the garden yields,
Flocks that whiten all the plain,
Yellow sheaves of ripen'd grain;
Lord, for these our souls shall raise
Grateful vows and solemn praise.

3.

Clouds that drop their fattening dews,
Suns that genial warmth diffuse,
All the plenty summer pours,
Autumn's rich o'erflowing stores;
Lord, for these our souls shall raise
Grateful vows and solemn praise.

4.

Peace, prosperity, and health,
Private bliss and public wealth,
Knowledge, with its gladdening streams,
Pure religion's holier beams;
Lord, for these our souls shall raise
Grateful vows and solemn praise.

HYMN 43. 6s. 4s.

GOD bless our native land!
Firm may she ever stand,

BAPTISM.

Through storm and night;
When the wild tempests rave,
Ruler of winds and wave,
Do thou our country save
  By thy great might.

2.

For her our prayer shall rise
To God, above the skies,
  On him we wait;
Thou who art ever nigh,
Guarding with watchful eye,
To thee aloud we cry,
  God save the State!

BAPTISM.

HYMN 44.   8s, 7s.

SAVIOUR, who thy flock art feeding,
  With the shepherd's kindest care,
All the feeble gently leading,
  While the lambs thy bosom share:

2.

Now, *these* little *ones* receiving,
  Fold *them* in thy gracious arm;
There, we know, thy word believing,
  Only there secure from harm.

3.

Never from thy pasture roving,
  Let *them* be the lion's prey;
Let thy tenderness, so loving,
  Keep *them* all life's dangerous way.

4.

Then, within thy fold eternal,
  Let *them* find a resting place;
Feed in pastures ever vernal,
  Drink the rivers of thy grace.

HYMN 45. 8s, 7s, 4s.

SAVIOUR, like a shepherd lead us,
  Much we need thy tender care;
In thy pleasant pastures feed us;
  For our use thy folds prepare;
    Blessèd Jesus!
  Thou hast bought us, thine we are.

2.

Thou hast promised to receive us,
  Poor and simple though we be;
Thou hast mercy to relieve us;
  Grace to cleanse, and power to free:
    Blessèd Jesus!
  Let us early turn to thee.

3.

Early let us seek thy favor,
  Early let us learn thy will;
Do thou, Lord, our only Saviour,
  With thy love our bosoms fill:
    Blessèd Jesus!
  Thou hast loved us—love us still.

HYMN 46. S. M.

SOLDIERS of Christ, arise,
  And put your armor on;

LORD'S SUPPER.

Strong in the strength which God supplies
Through his eternal Son.

2.
Strong in the Lord of hosts,
  And in his mighty power:
Who in the strength of Jesus trusts,
  Is more than conqueror.

3.
Stand, then, in his great might,
  With all his strength endued;
And take, to arm you for the fight,
  The panoply of God;

4.
That, having all things done,
  And all your conflicts past,
Ye may behold your victory won,
  And stand complete at last.

LORD'S SUPPER.
HYMN 47. L. M.

TO Jesus, our exalted Lord,
That name in heaven and earth adored,
Fain would our hearts and voices raise
A cheerful song of sacred praise.

2.
But all the notes which mortals know
Are weak, and languishing, and low;
Far, far above our humble songs,
The theme demands immortal tongues.

3.

Yet whilst around his board we meet,
And worship at his sacred feet,
O let our warm affections move
In glad returns of grateful love.

4.

Yes, Lord, we love, and we adore,
But long to know and love thee more,
And, whilst we take the bread and wine,
Desire to feed on joys divine.

HYMN 48. L. M.

MY God, and is thy table spread,
   And does thy cup with love o'erflow?
Thither be all thy children led,
   And let them thy sweet mercies know.

2.

O let thy table honor'd be,
   And furnish'd well with joyful guests:
And may each soul salvation see,
   That here its holy pledges tastes.

3.

Drawn by thy quickening grace,
   In countless numbers let them come;
And gather from their Father's board
   The bread that lives beyond the tomb.

4.

Nor let thy spreading Gospel rest,
   Till through the world thy truth has run;

Till with this bread all men be blest,
  Who see the light or feel the sun.

HYMN 49. C. M.

AND are we now brought near to God,
  Who once at distance stood?
And, to effect this glorious change,
  Did Jesus shed his blood?

2.
O for a song of ardent praise,
  To bear our souls above!
What should allay our lively hope,
  Or damp our flaming love?

3.
Then let us join the heavenly choirs,
  To praise our heavenly King:
O may that love which spread this board
  Inspire us while we sing:

4.
" Glory to God in highest strains,
  And to the earth be peace;
Good-will from heaven to men is come,
  And let it never cease."

HYMN 50. P. M.

BREAD of the world, in mercy broken,
  Wine of the soul, in mercy shed,
By whom the words of life were spoken,
  And in whose death our sins are dead:

2.

Look on the heart by sorrow broken,
   Look on the tears by sinners shed,
And be Thy feast to us the token
   That by Thy grace our souls are fed.

HYMN 51. C. M.

THOU, God, all glory, honor, power,
   Art worthy to receive;
Since all things by thy power were made,
   And by thy bounty live.

2.

And worthy is the Lamb, all power,
   Honor, and wealth to gain,
Glory and strength; who for our sins
   A sacrifice was slain.

3.

All worthy thou, who hast redeem'd
   And ransom'd us to God,
From every nation, every coast,
   By thy most precious blood.

4.

Blessing and honor, glory, power,
   By all in earth and heaven,
To him that sits upon the throne,
   And to the Lamb, be given.

HYMN 52. C. M.

TO our Redeemer's glorious name
   Awake the sacred song!
O may his love (immortal flame!)
   Tune every heart and tongue.

CONFIRMATION.

2.

His love what mortal thought can reach?
  What mortal tongue display?
Imagination's utmost stretch
  In wonder dies away.

3.

He left his radiant throne on high,
  Left the bright realms of bliss,
And came to earth to bleed and die!
  Was ever love like this?

4.

Dear Lord, while we adoring pay
  Our humble thanks to thee,
May every heart with rapture say,
  The Saviour died for me!

5.

O may the sweet, the blissful theme,
  Fill every heart and tongue;
Till strangers love thy charming name,
  And join the sacred song.

CONFIRMATION.

HYMN 53. 7s.

THINE for ever:—God of love,
  Hear us from thy throne above;
Thine for ever may we be,
Here and in eternity.

2.

Thine for ever:—Lord of life,
Shield us through our earthly strife:
Thou the life, the truth, the way,
Guide us to the realms of day.

3.

Thine for ever:—O how bless'd
They who find in thee their rest!
Saviour, guardian, heavenly friend,
O defend us to the end.

4.

Thine for ever:—thou our guide,
All our wants by thee supplied,
All our sins by thee forgiven,
Lead us, Lord, from earth to heaven.

HYMN 54. 6s. 4s.

MY faith looks up to thee,
 Thou Lamb of Calvary,
  Saviour divine!
Now hear me while I pray:
Take all my guilt away;
O let me from this day
  Be wholly thine.

2.

May thy rich grace impart
Strength to my fainting heart,
 My zeal inspire:

CONFIRMATION.

As thou hast died for me,
O may my love to thee
Pure, warm, and changeless be,
   A living fire.

3.

While life's dark maze I tread,
And griefs around me spread,
   Be thou my guide;
Bid darkness turn to day,
Wipe sorrow's tears away,
Nor let me ever stray
   From thee aside.

4.

When ends life's transient dream,
When death's cold, sullen stream
   Shall o'er me roll,
Blest Saviour, then in love,
Fear and distrust remove;
O bear me safe above,
   A ransom'd soul.

HYMN 55. 7s.

OFT in danger, oft in woe,
   Onward, Christians, onward go;
Fight the fight, maintain the strife,
Strengthen'd with the bread of life.

2.

Onward, Christians, onward go,
Join the war, and face the foe:

Will ye flee in danger's hour?
Know ye not your Captain's power?

3.

Let your drooping hearts be glad:
March, in heavenly armor clad:
Fight, nor think the battle long,
Victory soon shall tune your song.

4.

Let not sorrow dim your eye;
Soon shall every tear be dry;
Let not fears your course impede,
Great your strength, if great your need.

5.

Onward, then, in battle move,
More than conquerors ye shall prove;
Though opposed by many a foe,
Christian soldiers, onward go.

HYMN 56. P. M.

JUST as I am—without one plea,
But that thy blood was shed for me,
And that thou bid'st me come to thee,
  O Lamb of God, I come.

2.

Just as I am—and waiting not
To rid my soul of one dark blot;
To thee, whose blood can cleanse each spot,
  O Lamb of God, I come.

ORDINATION.

3.

Just as I am—though tossed about
With many a conflict, many a doubt
Fightings within, and fears without,
  O Lamb of God, I come.

4.

Just as I am—poor, wretched, blind;
Sight, riches, healing of the mind,
Yea, all I need, in thee to find,
  O Lamb of God, I come.

5.

Just as I am—thou wilt receive,
Wilt welcome, pardon, cleanse, relieve;
Because thy promise I believe,
  O Lamb of God, I come.

6.

Just as I am—thy love unknown
Has broken every barrier down;
Now, to be thine, yea, thine alone,
  O Lamb of God, I come.

ORDINATION.

HYMN 57. L. M.

FATHER of mercies bow thine ear,
  Attentive to our earnest prayer:
We plead for those who plead for thee;
Successful pleaders may they be.

2.
How great their work, how vast their charge;
Do thou their anxious souls enlarge:
Their best acquirements are our gain;
We share the blessings they obtain.

3.
Clothe, then, with energy divine,
Their words, and let those words be thine;
To them thy sacred truth reveal,
Suppress their fear, inflame their zeal.

4.
Teach them to sow the precious seed,
Teach them thy chosen flock to feed;
Teach them immortal souls to gain—
Souls that will well reward their pain.

5.
Let thronging multitudes around
Hear from their lips the joyful sound;
In humble strains thy grace implore,
And feel thy new-creating power.

6.
Let sinners break their massy chains,
Distressèd souls forget their pains;
Let light through distant realms be spread,
And Sion rear her drooping head.

HYMN 58. L. M.

GO forth, ye heralds, in my Name,
 Sweetly the Gospel trumpet sound;

ORDINATION.

The glorious jubilee proclaim,
  Where'er the human race is found.

2.

The joyful news to all impart,
  And teach them where salvation lies;
With care bind up the broken heart,
  And wipe the tears from weeping eyes.

3.

Be wise as serpents, where you go,
  But harmless as the peaceful dove;
And let your heaven-taught conduct show
  That ye're commission'd from above.

4.

Freely from me ye have received,
  Freely, in love, to others give:
Thus shall your doctrines be believed,
  And, by your labors, sinners live.

HYMN 59. L. M.

GO, speak of Jesus! of that love,
  Passing all bounds of human thought,
Which made him quit his throne above,
  With Godlike deep compassion fraught,
To save from death our ruined race,
Our guilt to purge, our path to trace.

2.

Go, speak of Jesus! of his power,
  As perfect God and perfect man,

Which day by day, and hour by hour,
  As he wrought out the wondrous plan,
Led him as God to save and heal,
As man to sympathize and feel.

3.

Go, speak of Jesus! of his grace,
  Receiving, pardoning, blessing all;
His holy, spotless life retrace,
  His words, his miracles recall;
The words he spoke, the truths he taught,
With life, eternal life, are fraught.

HYMN 60. L. M.

O SPIRIT of the living God!
  In all thy plenitude of grace,
Where'er the foot of man hath trod,
  Descend on our apostate race.

2.

Give tongues of fire and hearts of love,
  To preach the reconciling word;
Give power and unction from above,
  Whene'er the joyful sound is heard.

3.

Be darkness, at thy coming, light;
  Confusion, order in thy path;
Souls without strength inspire with might;
  Bid mercy triumph over wrath.

PRAISE.

4.

Convert the nations; far and nigh
  The triumphs of the cross record;
The name of Jesus glorify,
  Till every people call him Lord.

PRAISE.

HYMN 61. L. M.

O RENDER thanks to God above,
  The fountain of eternal love;
Whose mercy firm, through ages past,
Has stood, and shall for ever last.

2.

Who can his mighty deeds express,
Not only vast, but numberless?
What mortal eloquence can raise
His tribute of immortal praise.

3.

Extend to me that favor, Lord,
Thou to thy chosen dost afford;
When thou return'st to set them free,
Let thy salvation visit me.

4.

Let Israel's God be ever bless'd,
  His name eternally confess'd;
Let all his saints, with full accord,
Sing loud Amens: Praise ye the Lord.

HYMN 62.   C. M.

O FOR a heart to praise my God,
   A heart from sin set free!
A heart that's sprinkled with the blood
   So freely shed for me;

2.

A heart resigned, submissive, meek,
   My dear Redeemer's throne,
Where only Christ is heard to speak,
   Where Jesus reigns alone;

3.

An humble, lowly, contrite heart,
   Believing, true, and clean;
Which neither life nor death can part
   From him that dwells within;

4.

A heart in every thought renewed,
   And full of love divine,
Perfect, and right, and pure, and good—
   A copy, Lord, of thine!

5.

Thy nature, gracious Lord, impart;
   Come quickly from above;
Write thy new name upon my heart,
   Thy new, best name of Love.

HYMN 63.   7s.

MAGNIFY Jehovah's Name;
   For his mercies ever sure,

From eternity the same,
   To eternity endure.

2.
Let his ransom'd flock rejoice,
   Gather'd out of every land,
As the people of his choice,
   Pluck'd from the destroyer's hand.

3.
In the wilderness astray,
   In the lonely waste they roam,
Hungry, fainting by the way,
   Far from refuge, shelter, home:—

4.
To the Lord their God they cry;
   He inclines a gracious ear,
Sends deliverance from on high,
   Rescues them from all their fear:

5.
Them to pleasant lands he brings,
   Where the vine and olive grow;
Where, from verdant hills, the springs
   Through luxuriant valleys flow.

6.
O that men would praise the Lord,
   For his goodness to their race;
For the wonders of his word,
   And the riches of his grace.

HYMN 64. C. M.

O FOR a thousand tongues to sing
   My dear Redeemer's praise,

HYMNS.

The glories of my God and King,
　　The triumphs of his grace.

2.

Jesus—the name that charms our fears,
　　That bids our sorrows cease;
'Tis music in the sinner's ears,
　　'Tis life, and health, and peace.

3.

He breaks the power of inbred sin,
　　And sets the prisoner free;
His blood can make the foulest clean,
　　His blood availed for me.

4.

He speaks; and listening to his voice,
　　New life the dead receive;
The mournful broken hearts rejoice;
　　The humble poor believe.

5.

Hear him, ye deaf! His praise, ye dumb,
　　Your loosened tongues employ!
Ye blind, behold your Saviour come!
　　And leap, ye lame, for joy!

HYMN 65. L. M.

JEHOVAH reigns, let all the earth
　　In his just government rejoice;
Let all the lands, with sacred mirth,
　　In his applause unite their voice.

PRAISE.

2.

Darkness and cloud, of awful shade,
　His dazzling glory shroud in state;
Judgment and righteousness are made
　The habitation of his seat.

3.

For thou, O God, art seated high,
　Above earth's potentates enthroned;
Thou, Lord, unrivaled in the sky,
　Supreme by all the gods art owned.

HYMN 66. L. M.

SWEET is the work, my God, my King,
　To praise thy name, give thanks, and sing;
To show thy love by morning light,
And talk of all thy truth at night.

2.

Sweet is the day of sacred rest;
No mortal cares shall seize my breast;
O may my heart in tune be found,
Like David's harp of solemn sound.

3.

My heart shall triumph in the Lord,
And bless his works, and bless his word;
His works of grace, how bright they shine!
How deep his counsels, how divine!

4.

I then shall share a glorious part,
When grace hath well refined my heart,

And fresh supplies of joy are shed,
Like holy oil, to cheer my head.

5.

Then shall I see, and hear, and know,
All I desired or wished below;
And every power find sweet employ
In that eternal world of joy.

HYMN 67. 7s.

SONGS of praise the angels sang,
Heaven with hallelujahs rang,
When Jehovah's work begun,
When he spake, and it was done.

2.

Songs of praise awoke the morn
When the Prince of Peace was born;
Songs of praise arose when he
Captive led captivity.

3.

Heaven and earth must pass away:
Songs of praise shall crown that day.
God will make new heavens and earth:
Songs of praise shall hail their birth.

4.

Saints below, with heart and voice,
Still in songs of praise rejoice;
Learning here, by faith and love,
Songs of praise to sing above.

PRAISE.

5.
Borne upon their latest breath,
Songs of praise shall conquer death;
Then, amidst eternal joy,
Songs of praise their powers employ.

HYMN 68. L. M.

O COME, loud anthems let us sing,
Loud thanks to our Almighty King;
For we our voices high should raise,
When our salvation's rock we praise.

2.
Into his presence let us haste,
To thank him for his favors past;
To him address, in joyful songs,
The praise that to his Name belongs:

3.
O let us to his courts repair,
And bow with adoration there;
Down on our knees, devoutly, all,
Before the Lord, our Maker, fall.

4.
For he's our God, our Shepherd he,
His flock and pasture-sheep are we:
O then, ye faithful flock, to-day
His warning hear, his voice obey.

HYMN 69. 7s.

CHILDREN of the heavenly King,
As ye journey sweetly sing;

Sing your Saviour's worthy praise,
Glorious in his works and ways.

2.

We are travelling home to God,
In the way our fathers trod;
They are happy now, and we
Soon their happiness shall see.

3.

Banished once, by sin betray'd,
Christ our Advocate was made;
Pardon'd now, no more we roam,
Christ conducts us to our home.

4.

Lord, obediently we go,
Gladly leaving all below;
Only thou our Leader be,
And we still will follow thee.

HYMN 70. L. M.

BEFORE Jehovah's awful throne,
  Ye nations bow with sacred joy;
Know that the Lord is God alone,
  He can create, and he destroy.

2.

His sovereign power, without our aid,
  Made us of clay, and formed us men;
And when like wandering sheep we strayed,
  He brought us to his fold again.

3.

We'll crowd thy gates with thankful songs,
   High as the heavens our voices raise;
And earth, with her ten thousand tongues,
   Shall fill thy courts with sounding praise.

4.

Wide as the world is thy command,
   Vast as eternity thy love;
Firm as a rock thy truth must stand,
   When rolling years shall cease to move.

HYMN 71. 8s, 7s.

PART I.

GOD, my King, thy might confessing,
   Ever will I bless thy Name;
Day by day thy throne addressing,
   Still will I thy praise proclaim.

2.

Honor great our God befitteth;
   Who his majesty can reach?
Age to age his works transmitteth,
   Age to age his power shall teach.

3.

They shall talk of all thy glory,
   On thy might and greatness dwell,
Speak of thy dread acts the story,
   And thy deeds of wonder tell.

HYMNS.

4.

Nor shall fail from memory's treasure,
  Works by love and mercy wrought;
Works of love surpassing measure,
  Works of mercy passing thought.

5.

Full of kindness and compassion,
  Slow to anger, vast in love,
God is good to all creation;
  All his works his goodness prove.

PART II.

All thy works, O Lord, shall bless thee,
  Thee shall all thy saints adore;
King supreme shall they confess thee,
  And proclaim thy sovereign power.

2.

They thy might, all might excelling,
  Shall to all mankind make known;
And the brightness of thy dwelling,
  And the glories of thy throne.

3.

Ever, God of endless praises,
  Shall thy royal might remain;
Evermore thy brightness blazes,
  Ever lasts thy righteous reign.

4.

Them that fall the Lord protecteth,
  He sustains the bow'd and bent:
Every eye from thee expecteth,
  Fix'd on thee, its nourishment.

PRAISE.

PART III.

God is just in all he doeth,
 Kind is he in all his ways;
He his ready presence showeth,
 When a faithful servant prays.

2.

Who sincerely seek and fear him,
 He to them their wish shall give;
When they call, the Lord will hear them
 He will hear them and relieve.

3.

From Jehovah, all who prize him,
 Shall his saving health enjoy:
All the wicked who despise him,
 He will in their sin destroy.

4.

Still, Jehovah, thee confessing,
 Shall my tongue thy praise proclaim;
And may all mankind with blessing
 Ever hail thy holy Name.

HYMN 72. L. M.

AWAKE, my soul, to joyful lays,
 And sing thy great Redeemer's praise;
He justly claims a song from thee;
His loving kindness, O how free!

2.

He saw me ruined in the fall,
Yet loved me, notwithstanding all;

He saved me from my lost estate;
His loving kindness, O how great!

3.

Though numerous hosts of mighty foes,
Though earth and hell my way oppose,
He safely leads my soul along;
His loving kindness, O how strong!

4.

Often I feel my sinful heart
Prone from my Saviour to depart,
But though I oft have him forgot,
His loving kindness changes not.

5.

Soon shall I pass the gloomy vale,
Soon all my mortal powers must fail;
O may my last expiring breath
His loving kindness sing in death.

HYMN 73. L. M.

GREAT God, to thee my evening song
  With humble gratitude I raise:
O let thy mercy tune my tongue,
  And fill my heart with lively praise.

2.

My days unclouded as they pass,
  And every gently rolling hour,
Are monuments of wondrous grace,
  And witness to thy love and power.

PRAISE.

3.

And yet this thoughtless, wretched heart,
Too oft regardless of thy love.
Ungrateful, can from thee depart.
And from the path of duty rove.

4.

Seal my forgiveness in the blood
Of Jesus; his dear name alone
I plead for pardon, gracious God,
And kind acceptance at thy throne.

5.

Let this blest hope my eyelids close;
With sleep refresh my feeble frame;
Safe in thy care may I repose,
And wake with praises to thy name.

HYMN 74. 8s, 7s.

LORD, with glowing heart I'd praise thee,
For the bliss thy love bestows:
For the pardoning grace that saves me,
And the peace that from it flows:
Help, O God, my weak endeavor;
This dull soul to rapture raise:
Thou must light the flame, or never
Can my love be warmed to praise.

2.

Praise, my soul, the God that sought thee,
Wretched wanderer, far astray:

Found thee lost, and kindly brought thee
   From the paths of death away;
Praise, with love's devoutest feeling,
   Him who saw thy guilt-born fear,
And, the light of hope revealing,
   Bade the blood-stain'd cross appear.

3.

Lord, this bosom's ardent feeling
   Vainly would my lips express:
Low before thy footstool kneeling,
   Deign thy suppliant's prayer to bless:
Let thy grace, my soul's chief treasure,
   Love's pure flame within me raise;
And, since words can never measure,
   Let my life show forth thy praise.

HYMN 75. L. M.

GLORY to thee, my God, this night,
For all the blessings of the light;
Keep me, O keep me, King of kings,
Beneath thy own Almighty wings.

2.

Forgive me, Lord, for thy dear Son,
The ills that I this day have done;
That with the world, myself, and thee,
I, ere I sleep, at peace may be.

3.

Teach me to live, that I may dread
The grave as little as my bed;

Teach me to die, that so I may
Triumphing rise at the last day.

4.

O let my soul on thee repose,
And may sweet sleep mine eyelids close;
Sleep that shall me more vigorous make,
To serve my God when I awake.

5.

Praise God, from whom all blessings flow;
Praise him, all creatures here below;
Praise him above, ye heavenly host,
Praise Father, Son, and Holy Ghost.

HYMN 76. S. M.

COME, ye that love the Lord,
    And let your joys be known;
Join in a song with sweet accord,
    And thus surround the throne.

2.

Let those refuse to sing
    That never knew our God,
But children of the heavenly King
    May speak their joys abroad.

3.

The God of heaven is ours,
    Our Father and our love;
His care shall guard life's fleeting hours,
    Then waft our souls above.

4.

There shall we see his face,
  And never, never sin;
There, from the rivers of his grace,
  Drink endless pleasures in.

5.

Children of grace have found
  Glory begun below:
Celestial fruits on earthly ground
  From faith and hope may grow.

HYMN 77. C. M.

WHEN all thy mercies, O my God,
  My rising soul surveys,
Transported with the view, I'm lost
  In wonder, love, and praise.

2.

O how shall words with equal warmth
  The gratitude declare
That glows within my ravish'd heart?
  But thou canst read it there.

3.

Ten thousand thousand precious gifts
  My daily thanks employ;
Nor is the least a cheerful heart,
  That tastes those gifts with joy.

4.

Through every period of my life
  Thy goodness I'll pursue;

PRAISE.

And after death, in distant worlds,
  The glorious theme renew.

5.

When nature fails, and day and night
  Divide thy works no more,
My ever grateful heart, O Lord,
  Thy mercy shall adore.

6.

Through all eternity, to thee
  A joyful song I'll raise;
But oh! eternity's too short
  To utter all thy praise.

HYMN 78. L. M.

FROM all that dwell below the skies
  Let the Creator's praise arise;
Jehovah's glorious name be sung
Through every land, by every tongue.

2.

Eternal are thy mercies, Lord,
And truth eternal is thy word:
Thy praise shall sound from shore to shore,
Till suns shall rise and set no more.

HYMN 79. L. M.

MY God, how endless is thy love!
  Thy gifts are every evening new;
And morning mercies from above
  Gently distill, like early dew.

2.

Thou spread'st the curtains of the night,
　Great Guardian of my sleeping hours;
Thy sovereign word restores the light,
　And quickens all my drowsy powers.

3.

I yield my powers to thy command,
　To thee I consecrate my days;
Perpetual blessings from thy hand
　Demand perpetual songs of praise.

HYMN 80.　8s, 7s.

COME, thou Fount of every blessing,
　Tune my heart to sing thy grace;
Streams of mercy, never ceasing,
　Call for songs of loudest praise:
Teach me the melodious measures
　Sung by seraph-choirs above,
While I tell the boundless treasures
　Of my Lord's unchanging love.

2.

Here I raise my Ebenezer;
　Hither, by thy help, I'm come;
And I hope, through thy good pleasure,
　Safely to arrive at home.
Jesus sought me when a stranger,
　Wandering from the fold of God;
He, to rescue me from danger,
　Interposed his precious blood.

3.

O, to grace how great a debtor
  Daily I'm constrained to be!
Let thy grace now, like a fetter,
  Bind my wandering heart to thee.
Prone to wander—Lord, I feel it—
  Prone to leave the God I love;
Here's my heart, O take and seal it,
  Seal it from thy courts above.

HYMN 81. C. M.

THROUGH all the changing scenes of life,
  In trouble and in joy,
The praises of my God shall still
  My heart and tongue employ.

2.

Of his deliverance I will boast,
  Till all that are distressed
From my example comfort take,
  And charm their griefs to rest.

3.

O magnify the Lord with me,
  With me exalt his name;
When in distress to him I call'd,
  He to my rescue came.

4.

The angel of the Lord encamps
  Around the good and just;

Deliverance he affords to all
  Who on his succor trust.

5.

O make but trial of his love,
  Experience will decide
How blest are they, and only they,
  Who in his truth confide.

6.

Fear him, ye saints; and you will then
  Have nothing else to fear;
Make you his service your delight,
  Your wants shall be his care.

HYMN 82. II. M.

YE boundless realms of joy,
  Exalt your Maker's fame;
His praise your song employ
  Above the starry frame:
    Your voices raise,
    Ye cherubim
    And seraphim,
    To sing his praise.

2.

Thou moon, that rul'st the night,
  And sun, that guid'st the day,
Ye glittering stars of light,
  To him your homage pay:
    His praise declare,
    Ye heavens above,
    And clouds that move
    In liquid air.

3.

Let them adore the Lord,
  And praise his holy name,
By whose almighty word
  They all from nothing came;
    And all shall last,
    From changes free;
    His firm decree
      Stands ever fast.

HYMN 83. S. M.

O BLESS the Lord, my soul,
  His grace to thee proclaim;
And all that is within me, join
  To bless his holy Name.

2.

O bless the Lord, my soul,
  His mercies bear in mind;
Forget not all his benefits,
  Who is to thee so kind.

3.

He pardons all thy sins,
  Prolongs thy feeble breath;
He healeth thine infirmities,
  And ransoms thee from death.

4.

He feeds thee with his love,
  Upholds thee with his truth;
And, like the eagles, he renews
  The vigor of thy youth.

5.

Then bless the Lord, my soul,
　His grace, his love proclaim;
Let all that is within me, join
　To bless his holy Name.

PRAYER.

HYMN 84.　L. M.

FROM every stormy wind that blows,
　From every swelling tide of woes,
There is a calm, a sure retreat;
'Tis found beneath the mercy-seat.

2.

There is a place where Jesus sheds
The oil of gladness on our heads—
A place than all beside more sweet,
It is the blood-stained mercy-seat.

3.

There is a spot where spirits blend,
Where friend holds fellowship with friend;
Though sunder'd far, by faith they meet
Around one common mercy-seat.

4.

There, there, on eagles' wings we soar,
And time and sense seem all no more;
And heaven comes down, our souls to greet,
And glory crowns the mercy-seat.

HYMN 85. 8s.

INSPIRER and hearer of prayer,
　Thou shepherd and guardian of thine,
My all to thy covenant care,
　I, sleeping or waking, resign.

2.

If thou art my shield and my sun,
　The night is no darkness to me;
And, fast as my minutes roll on,
　They bring me but nearer to thee.

3.

A sovereign protector I have,
　Unseen, yet forever at hand;
Unchangeably faithful to save,
　Almighty to rule and command.

4.

His smiles and his comforts abound,
　His grace, as the dew, shall descend:
And walls of salvation surround
　The soul he delights to defend.

HYMN 86. C. M.

WHILE Thee I seek, protecting Power,
　Be my vain wishes still'd:
And may this consecrated hour
　With better hopes be filled.

2.

Thy love the power of thought bestow'd,
　To Thee my thoughts would soar;

Thy mercy o'er my life has flowed,
  That mercy I adore.

3.

In each event of life, how clear
  Thy ruling hand I see:
Each blessing to my soul more dear,
  Because conferr'd by Thee.

4.

In every joy that crowns my days,
  In every pain I bear,
My heart shall find delight in praise,
  Or seek relief in prayer.

5.

When gladness wings my favor'd hour,
  Thy love my thoughts shall fill;
Resign'd, when storms of sorrow lower,
  My soul shall meet Thy will.

6.

My lifted eye, without a tear,
  The gathering storm shall see;
My steadfast heart shall know no fear,
  That heart will rest on Thee.

HYMN 87. C. M.

PRAYER is the soul's sincere desire,
  Uttered or unexpressed:
The motion of a hidden fire
  That trembles in the breast.

PRAYER.

2.
Prayer is the burden of a sigh,
  The falling of a tear;
The upward glancing of an eye
  When none but God is near.

3.
Prayer is the simplest form of speech
  That infant lips can try;
Prayer, the sublimest strains that reach
  The Majesty on high.

4.
Prayer is the contrite sinner's voice,
  Returning from his ways;
While angels in their songs rejoice,
  And cry, "Behold, he prays."

5.
Prayer is the Christian's vital breath,
  The Christian's native air;
His watchword at the gates of death,
  He enters heaven with prayer.

6.
The saints, in prayer, appear as one,
  In word, and deed, and mind;
While with the Father and the Son
  Sweet fellowship they find.

7.
Nor prayer is made by man alone;
  The Holy Spirit pleads;
And Jesus on the eternal throne
  For sinners intercedes.

8.

O thou, by whom we come to God,
  The life, the truth, the way,
The path of prayer thyself hast trod;
  Lord, teach us how to pray.

HYMN 88. C. M.

APPROACH, my soul, the mercy-seat,
  Where Jesus answers prayer;
There humbly fall before his feet,
  For none can perish there.

2.
Thy promise is my only plea,
  With this I venture nigh;
Thou callest burden'd souls to thee,
  And such, O Lord, am I.

3.
Bow'd down beneath a load of sin,
  By Satan sorely press'd,
By war without, and fears within,
  I come to thee for rest.

4.
Be thou my shield and hiding-place;
  That, shelter'd near thy side,
I may my fierce accuser face,
  And tell him thou hast died!

5.
O wondrous love, to bleed and die,
  To bear the cross and shame,

That guilty sinners, such as I,
  Might plead thy gracious name.

HYMN 89. S. M.

JESUS, my strength, my hope,
  On thee I cast my care,
With humble confidence look up.
  And know thou hear'st my prayer:
Give me on thee to wait,
  Till I can all things do—
On thee, almighty to create,
  Almighty to renew.

2.

Give me a sober mind,
  A self-renouncing will,
That tramples down and casts behind
  The baits of pleasing ill:
A soul inured to pain,
  To hardship, grief, and loss,
Ready to take up and sustain
  The consecrated cross.

3.

Give me a godly fear,
  A quick, discerning eye,
That looks to thee when sin is near,
  And sees the tempter fly:
A spirit still prepared,
  And armed with jealous care,
For ever standing on its guard,
  And watching unto prayer.

4.

I rest upon thy word,
 The promise is for me;
My succor and salvation, Lord,
 Shall surely come from thee;
But let me still abide,
 Nor from my hope remove,
Till thou my patient spirit guide
 Into thy perfect love.

THE LORD'S DAY.

HYMN 90. S. M.

THIS is the day of light:
 Let there be light to-day;
O Day-Spring, rise upon our night,
 And chase its gloom away.

2.

This is the day of rest:
 Our failing strength renew;
On weary brain and troubled breast
 Shed thou thy freshening dew.

3.

This is the day of peace:
 Thy peace our spirits fill;
Bid thou the blasts of discord cease,
 The waves of strife be still.

4.

This is the day of prayer:
 Let earth to heaven draw near;

THE LORD'S DAY.

Lift up our hearts to seek thee there;
   Come down to meet us here.

5.

This is the first of days:
   Send forth thy quickening breath,
And wake dead souls to love and praise,
   O Vanquisher of death!

HYMN 91.   8s, 7s, 4s.

IN thy name, O Lord, assembling,
   We, thy people, now draw near;
Teach us to rejoice with trembling:
   Speak, and let thy servants hear;
      Hear with meekness,
   Hear thy word with godly fear.

2.

While our days on earth are lengthened,
   May we give them, Lord, to thee,
Cheered by hope, and daily strengthened,
   May we run, nor weary be,
      Till thy glory
   Without clouds in heaven we see.

3.

Then in worship, purer, sweeter,
   Thee thy people shall adore,
Tasting of enjoyment greater
   Far than thought conceived before.
      Full enjoyment,
   Full, unmixed, and evermore.

HYMN 92. L. M.

HAPPY the man that finds the grace,
The blessing of God's chosen race,
The wisdom coming from above,
The faith that sweetly works by love.

2.
Happy, beyond description, he
Who knows "the Saviour died for me!"
The gift unspeakable obtains,
And heavenly understanding gains.

3.
Wisdom divine! who tells the price
Of wisdom's costly merchandise?
Wisdom to silver we prefer,
And gold is dross compared with her.

4.
Her hands are fill'd with length of days,
True riches and immortal praise;
Riches of Christ on all bestow'd,
And honor that descends from God.

5.
To purest joys she all invites,
Chaste, holy, spiritual delights:
Her ways are ways of pleasantness,
And all her flowery paths are peace.

6.
Happy the man who wisdom gains:
Thrice happy who his guest retains:
He owns, and shall forever own,
Wisdom, and Christ, and heaven are one.

THE LORD'S DAY.

HYMN 93. L. M.

WITH one consent let all the earth
  To God their cheerful voices raise;
Glad homage pay with awful mirth,
  And sing before him songs of praise.

2.
Convinced that he is God alone,
  From whom both we and all proceed:
We, whom he chooses for his own,
  The flock that he vouchsafes to feed.

3.
O enter then his temple gate,
  Thence to his courts devoutly press;
And still your grateful hymns repeat,
  And still his name with praises bless.

4.
For he's the Lord, supremely good,
  His mercy is for ever sure:
His truth, which always firmly stood,
  To endless ages shall endure.

HYMN 94. S. M.

WELCOME, sweet day of rest,
  That saw the Lord arise;
Welcome to this reviving breast,
  And these rejoicing eyes.

2.
The King himself comes near
  And feasts his saints to-day;

Here may we sit, and see him here,
  And love, and praise, and pray.

3.

One day of prayer and praise
  Where Jesus is within,
Is sweeter than ten thousand days
  Of pleasurable sin.

4.

My willing soul would stay
  In such a frame as this,
And wait to hail the brighter day
  Of everlasting bliss.

HYMN 95. C. M.

LORD! in the morning thou shalt hear
  My voice ascending high;
To thee will I direct my prayer,
  To thee lift up mine eye:

2.

Up to the hills, where Christ is gone
  To plead for all his saints,
Presenting at his Father's throne
  Our songs and our complaints.

3.

Thou art a God before whose sight
  The wicked shall not stand;
Sinners shall ne'er be thy delight,
  Nor dwell at thy right hand.

THE LORD'S DAY.

4
But to thy house will I resort,
 To taste thy mercies there;
I will frequent thy holy court,
 And worship in thy fear.

5.
O may thy Spirit guide my feet
 In ways of righteousness,
Make every path of duty straight,
 And plain before my face.

HYMN 96. C. M.

O GOD of hosts, the mighty Lord,
 How lovely is the place
Where thou, enthroned in glory, show'st
 The brightness of thy face!

2.
My longing soul faints with desire
 To view thy blest abode;
My panting heart and flesh cry out
 For thee, the living God.

3.
Thrice happy they whose choice has thee
 Their sure protection made,
Who long to tread the sacred ways
 That to thy dwelling lead.

4.
Thus they proceed from strength to strength,
 And still approach more near,

Till all on Sion's holy mount
  Before their God appear.

5.

For God, who is our sun and shield,
  Will grace and glory give;
And no good thing will he withhold
  From them that justly live.

6.

Thou God, whom heavenly hosts obey,
  How highly bless'd is he
Whose hope and trust, securely placed,
  Are still reposed on thee!

HYMN 97. L. M.

ANOTHER six days' work is done,
  Another Lord's day is begun;
Return, my soul, unto thy rest,
Enjoy the day thy God hath blest.

2.

O that our thoughts and thanks may rise
As greatful incense to the skies!
And draw from heaven that calm repose,
Which none but he who feels it knows.

3.

That heavenly calm within the breast!
It is the pledge of that dear rest
Which for the Church of God remains,
The end of cares, the end of pains.

THE LORD'S DAY.

4.
In holy duties, let the day,
In holy pleasures, pass away:
How sweet a Sabbath thus to spend,
In hope of one that ne'er shall end!

HYMN 98. H. M.

AWAKE, ye saints, awake,
  And hail this sacred day;
In loftiest songs of praise
  Your joyful homage pay:
Welcome the day that God hath blest,
The type of heaven's eternal rest.

2.
On this auspicious morn
  The Lord of life arose;
He burst the bars of death,
  And vanquish'd all our foes:
And now he pleads our cause above,
And reaps the fruits of all his love.

3.
All hail, triumphant Lord!
  Heaven with hosannas rings,
And earth, in humbler strains,
  Thy praise responsive sings:
Worthy the Lamb that once was slain,
Through endless years to live and reign.

4.
Great King, gird on thy sword,
  Ascend thy conquering car;

While justice, truth, and love
  Maintain thy glorious war:
This day let sinners own thy sway,
And rebels cast their arms away.

NEW YEAR.

HYMN 99. C. M.

O GOD, our help in ages past,
  Our hope for years to come,
Our shelter from the stormy blast,
  And our eternal home:

2.

Under the shadow of thy throne
  Thy saints have dwelt secure;
Sufficient is thine arm alone,
  And our defense is sure.

3.

Before the hills in order stood,
  Or earth received her frame,
From everlasting thou art God,
  To endless years the same.

4.

A thousand ages in thy sight
  Are like an evening gone;
Short as the watch that ends the night
  Before the rising sun.

5.

Time, like an ever-rolling stream,
  Bears all its sons away:

NEW YEAR.

They fly forgotten, as a dream
  Dies at the opening day.

6.

O God, our help in ages past,
  Our hope for years to come,
Be thou our guard while life shall last,
  And our eternal home.

HYMN 100. L. M.

THE God of life, whose constant care
  With blessing crowns each opening year,
My scanty span doth still prolong,
And wakes anew mine annual song.

2.

Thy children, panting to be gone,
May bid the tide of time roll on,
To land them on that happy shore
Where years and death are known no more.

3.

No more fatigue, no more distress,
Nor sin, nor hell, shall reach that place;
No groans to mingle with the songs,
Resounding from immortal tongues:

4.

No more alarms from ghostly foes;
No cares to break the long repose;
No midnight shade, no clouded sun,
But sacred, high, eternal noon.

5.

O long-expected year! begin;
Dawn on this world of woe and sin;
Fain would we leave this weary road,
And sleep in death, to rest with God.

HYMN 101.   7s.

WHILE with ceaseless course the sun
   Hasted through the former year.
Many souls their race have run,
   Never more to meet us here:
Fixed in an eternal state,
   They have done with all below:
We a little longer wait,
   But how little, none can know.

2.

As the wingèd arrow flies
   Speedily the mark to find;
As the lightning from the skies
   Darts, and leaves no trace behind;
Swiftly thus our fleeting days
   Bears us down life's rapid stream;
Upward, Lord, our spirits raise;
   All below is but a dream.

3.

Thanks for mercies past receive;
   Pardon of our sins renew;
Teach us henceforth how to live
   With eternity in view:
Bless thy word to young and old;
Fill us with a Saviour's love;

And when life's short tale is told,
May we dwell with thee above.

HYMN 102. C. M.

AS o'er the past my memory strays,
  Why heaves the secret sigh?
'Tis that I mourn departed days,
  Still unprepared to die.

2.
The world and worldly things belov'd,
  My anxious thoughts employ'd;
And time unhallow'd, unimproved,
  Presents a fearful void

3.
Yet holy Father, wild despair
  Chase from my laboring breast;
Thy grace it is which prompts the prayer,
  That grace can do the rest.

4.
My life's brief remnant all be Thine;
  And when Thy sure decree
Bids me this fleeting breath resign,
  O speed my soul to Thee.

COMMUNION OF SAINTS.

HYMN 103. S. M.

BLEST be the tie that binds
  Our hearts in Jesus' love;
The fellowship of Christian minds
  Is like to that above.

2.

Before our Father's throne
  We pour united prayers;
Our fears, our hopes, our aims are one;
  Our comforts and our cares.

3.

We share our mutual woes,
  Our mutual burdens bear;
And often for each other flows
  The sympathizing tear.

4.

When we at death must part,
  Not like the world's, our pain:
But one in Christ, and one in heart,
  We part to meet again.

5.

From sorrow, toil, and pain,
  And sin, we shall be free;
And perfect love and friendship reign
  Throughout eternity.

HYMN 104. C. M.

COME, let us join our friends above
  That have made sure the prize,
And on the eagle wings of love
  To joys celestial rise.

2.

Let all the saints terrestrial sing,
  With those to glory gone:
For all the servants of our King
  In earth and heaven are one.

COMMUNION OF SAINTS.

3.
One family, we dwell in him,
  One Church, above, beneath:
Though now divided by the stream,
  The narrow stream of death.

4.
One army of the living God,
  To his command we bow:
Part of his host have cross'd the flood,
  And part are crossing now.

5.
Our spirits, too, shall quickly join,
  Like theirs, with glory crown'd,
And shout to see our Captain's sign,
  To hear his trumpet sound.

6.
Then, Lord of hosts, be thou our guide,
  And we, at thy command,
Through waves that part on either side,
  Shall reach the blessèd land.

HYMN 105. C. M.

LO! what a cloud of witnesses
  Encompass us around!
Men once, like us, with suffering tried,
  But now with glory crown'd.

2.
Let us, with zeal like theirs inspired,
  Strive in the Christian race;
And, freed from every weight of sin,
  Their holy footsteps trace.

3.

Behold a witness nobler still,
  Who trod affliction's path—
Jesus, the Author, Finisher,
  Rewarder of our faith:

4.

He, for the joy before him set,
  And moved by pitying love,
Endured the cross, despised the shame,
  And now he reigns above.

5.

Thither, forgetting things behind,
  Press we, to God's right hand;
There, with the Saviour and his saints,
  Triumphantly to stand.

HYMN 106. C. M.

NOT to the terrors of the Lord,
  The tempest, fire, and smoke:
Not to the thunder of that word
  Which God on Sinai spoke;

2.

But we are come to Sion's hill,
  The city of our God;
Where milder words declare his will,
  And spread his love abroad.

3.

Behold th' innumerable host
  Of angels clothed in light:
Behold the spirits of the just,
  Whose faith is changed to sight.

4.

Behold the bless'd assembly there,
  Whose names are writ in heaven:
Hear God, the judge of all, declare
  Their sins, through Christ, forgiven.

5.

Angels, and living saints and dead,
  But one communion make:
All join in Christ, their living Head,
  And of his love partake.

HOLY SCRIPTURES.

HYMN 107.   C. M.

FATHER of mercies! in thy word
  What endless glory shines!
For ever be thy name adored
  For these celestial lines.

2.

Here the Redeemer's welcome voice
  Spreads heavenly peace around;
And life and everlasting joys
  Attend the blissful sound.

3.

O may these heavenly pages be
  My ever dear delight;
And still new beauties may I see,
  And still increasing light.

4.

Divine Instructor, gracious Lord,
  Be thou for ever near:
Teach me to love thy sacred word,
  And view my Saviour there.

HYMN 108. C. M.

GOD'S perfect law converts the soul,
  Reclaims from false desires;
With sacred wisdom his sure word
  The ignorant inspires.

2.

The statutes of the Lord are just,
  And bring sincere delight;
His pure commands, in search of truth,
  Assist the feeblest sight.

3.

His perfect worship here is fix'd,
  On sure foundations laid;
His equal laws are in the scales
  Of truth and justice weigh'd;

4.

Of more esteem than golden mines,
  Or gold refined with skill;
More sweet than honey, or the drops
  That from the comb distill.

5.

My trusty counsellors they are,
  And friendly warning give:

Divine rewards attend on those
Who by thy precepts live.

HYMN 109. C. M.

A GLORY gilds the sacred page,
  Majestic like the sun:
It gives a light to every age:
  It gives, but borrows none.

2.

The Hand that gave it still supplies
  The gracious light and heat:
His truths upon the nations rise;
  They rise, but never set.

3.

Let everlasting thanks be thine,
  For such a bright display
As makes a world of darkness shine
  With beams of heavenly day.

4.

My heart with early zeal began
  Thy statutes to obey;
And, till my course of life is done,
  Shall keep thine upright way.

5.

My soul rejoices to pursue
  The steps of him I love,
Till glory break upon my view
  In brighter worlds above.

HEAVEN.

HYMN 110. C. M.

THERE is a land of pure delight,
  Where saints immortal reign;
Infinite day excludes the night,
  And pleasures banish pain.

2.

There everlasting spring abides,
  And never-withering flowers;
Death, like a narrow sea, divides
  This heavenly land from ours.

3.

Sweet fields beyond the swelling flood
  Stand dressed in living green;
So to the Jews old Canaan stood,
  While Jordan rolled between.

4.

But timorous mortals start and shrink
  To cross this narrow sea;
And linger, shivering, on the brink,
  And fear to launch away.

5.

O could we make our doubts remove,
  Those gloomy doubts that rise,
And see the Canaan that we love
  With unbeclouded eyes;

6.

Could we but climb where Moses stood,
  And view the landscape o'er,

Not Jordan's stream, nor death's cold flood,
  Should fright us from the shore.

HYMN 111. 7s, 6s.

RISE, my soul, and stretch thy wings,
  Thy better portion trace;
Rise, from transitory things,
  Towards heaven, thy destined place:
Sun, and moon, and stars decay,
  Time shall soon this earth remove;
Rise, my soul, and haste away
  To seats prepared above.

2.

Cease, my soul, O cease to mourn,
  Press onward to the prize;
Soon thy Saviour will return,
  To take thee to the skies:
There is everlasting peace,
  Rest, enduring rest in heaven;
There will sorrow ever cease,
  And crowns of joy be given.

HYMN 112. C. M.

WHEN I can read my title clear
  To mansions in the skies,
I'll bid farewell to every fear,
  And wipe my weeping eyes.

2.

Should earth against my soul engage,
  And fiery darts be hurl'd,

Then I can smile at Satan's rage,
  And face a frowning world.

3.

Let cares like a wild deluge come,
  Let storms of sorrow fall;
So I but safely reach my home,
  My God, my heaven my all:

4.

There, anchor'd safe, my weary soul
  Shall find eternal rest;
Nor storms shall beat, nor billows roll
  Across my peaceful breast.

HYMN 113. 11s.

'MID scenes of confusion and creature
    complaints,
How sweet to my soul is communion with
    saints;
To find at the banquet of mercy there's
    room,
And feel in the presence of Jesus at home.

Home, home, sweet, sweet home,
Prepare me, dear Saviour, for glory, my
    home.

2.

Sweet bonds that unite all the children of
    peace!
And thrice precious Jesus, whose love
    cannot cease;

HEAVEN.

Though oft from thy presence in sadness
  I roam,
I long to behold thee in glory at home.

3.

Whate'er thou deniest, oh, give me thy
  grace,
The Spirit's sure witness, and smiles of
  thy face;
Endue me with patience to wait at thy
  throne,
And find, even now, a sweet foretaste of
  home.

4.

I long, dearest Lord, in thy beauties to
  shine;
No more as an exile in sorrow to pine;
And in thy dear image arise from the
  tomb,
With glorified millions to praise thee at
  home.

HYMN 114. P. M.

HARK! hark, my soul! Angelic songs
  are swelling
  O'er earth's green fields and ocean's
    wave-beat shore:
How sweet the truth those blessèd strains
  are telling
  Of that new life when sin shall be no
    more!

Angels of Jesus,
  Angels of light,
Singing to welcome
  The pilgrims of the night.

2.

Onward we go, for still we hear them singing,
  "Come, weary souls, for Jesus bids you come;"
And through the dark, its echoes sweetly ringing,
  The music of the Gospel leads us home.
    Angels of Jesus,
      Angels of light,
    Singing to welcome
      The pilgrims of the night.

3.

Far, far away, like bells at evening pealing,
  The voice of Jesus sounds o'er land and sea,
And laden souls, by thousands, meekly stealing,
  Kind Shepherd, turn their weary steps to thee.
    Angels of Jesus,
      Angels of light,
    Singing to welcome
      The pilgrims of the night.

HEAVEN.

4.

Rest comes at length, though life be long
 and dreary,
The day must dawn and darksome night
 be past;
All journeys end in welcome to the weary,
 And heaven, the heart's true home, will
 come at last.
  Angels of Jesus,
   Angels of light,
  Singing to welcome
   The pilgrims of the night.

5.

Angels, sing on! your faithful watches
 keeping;
Sing us sweet fragments of the songs
 above;
Till morning's joy shall end the night of
 weeping,
And life's long shadows break in cloud-
 less love.
  Angels of Jesus,
   Angels of light,
  Singing to welcome
   The pilgrims of the night.

HYMN 115. 7s, 6s.

FOR thee, O dear, dear Country,
 Mine eyes their vigils keep;
For very love, beholding
 Thy happy name, they weep;

The mention of thy glory
  Is unction to the breast,
And medicine in sickness,
  And love, and life, and rest.

2.

O one, O only mansion!
  O Paradise of Joy!
Where tears are ever banished,
  And smiles have no alloy;
The Lamb is all thy splendor;
  The Crucified thy praise;
His laud and benediction
  Thy ransomed people raise.

3.

With jasper glow thy bulwarks,
  Thy streets with emeralds blaze;
The sardius and the topaz
  Unite in thee their rays;
Thine ageless walls are bonded
  With amethyst unpriced;
The saints build up its fabric,
  And the corner stone is Christ.

4.

Thou hast no shore, fair ocean!
  Thou hast no time, bright day!
Dear fountain of refreshment
  To pilgrims far away!
Upon the Rock of Ages
  They raise thy holy tower;
Thine is the victor's laurel,
  And thine the golden dower.

HYMN 116. 7s, 6s.

JERUSALEM the golden!
  With milk and honey blest,
Beneath thy contemplation
  Sink heart and voice opprest.
I know not, oh! I know not
  What joys await us there;
What radiancy of glory,
  What bliss beyond compare!

2.

They stand, those halls of Sion,
  All jubilant with song,
And bright with many an angel,
  And all the martyr throng:
The Prince is ever in them,
  The daylight is serene,
The pastures of the blessèd
  Are decked in glorious sheen.

3.

There is the throne of David,
  And there, from care released,
The shout of them that triumph,
  The song of them that feast;
And they, who with their Leader
  Have conquered in the fight,
Forever and forever
  Are clad in robes of white.

4.

O sweet and blessed country,
  The home of God's elect!

O sweet and blessèd country,
  That eager hearts expect!
Jesus, in mercy bring us
  To that dear land of rest;
Who art, with God the Father,
  And Spirit, ever blest.

HYMN 117. C. M.

O MOTHER dear, Jerusalem!
  When shall I come to thee?
When shall my sorrows have an end?
  Thy joys when shall I see?

2.
O happy harbor of God's saints!
  O sweet and pleasant soil!
In thee no sorrow can be found,
  Nor grief, nor care, nor toil.

3.
No murky cloud o'ershadows thee,
  Nor gloom, nor darksome night;
But every soul shines as the sun;
  For God himself gives light.

4.
O my sweet home, Jerusalem!
  Thy joys when shall I see?
The King that sitteth on thy throne
  In his felicity?

5.
Thy gardens and thy goodly walks
  Continually are green,

HEAVEN.

Where grow such sweet and pleasant flowers
As nowhere else are seen.

6.

Right through thy streets, with pleasing sound,
The living waters flow,
And on the banks, on either side,
The trees of life do grow.

7.

Those trees each month yield ripen'd fruit,
Forevermore they spring,
And all the nations of the earth
To thee their honors bring.

HYMN 118. C. P. M.

WITH joy shall I behold the day
That calls my willing soul away,
To dwell among the blest:
For, lo! my great Redeemer's power
Unfolds the everlasting door,
And points me to his rest

2.

E'en now, to my expecting eyes,
The heaven-built towers of Salem rise;
Their glory I survey;
I view her mansions that contain
The angel host, a beauteous train,
And shine with cloudless day.

3.

Thither, from earth's remotest end,
All the redeem'd of God ascend,
  Borne on immortal wing;
There, crown'd with everlasting joy,
In ceaseless hymns their tongues employ,
  Before th' Almighty King.

4.

Mother of cities! o'er thy head
Bright peace, with healing wings outspread,
For evermore shall dwell:
Let me, blest seat! my name behold
Among thy citizens enroll'd,
  And bid the world farewell.

HYMN 119. C. M.

JERUSALEM, my happy home,
  Name ever dear to me,
When shall my labors have an end
  In joy, and peace, and thee?

2.

When shall these eyes thy heaven-built walls
  And pearly gates behold?
Thy bulwarks, with salvation strong,
  And streets of shining gold?

3.

There happier bowers than Eden's bloom,
  Nor sin nor sorrow know:

HEAVEN.

Blest seats! through rude and stormy scenes,
　I onward press to you.

4.

Why should I shrink from pain and woe,
　Or feel at death dismay?
I've Canaan's goodly land in view,
　And realms of endless day.

5.

Apostles, martyrs, prophets, there
　Around my Saviour stand:
And soon my friends in Christ below
　Will join the glorious band.

6.

Jerusalem, my happy home,
　My soul still pants for thee;
Then shall my labors have an end,
　When I thy joys shall see.

HYMN 120. S. M.

FOR ever with the Lord!
　Amen, so let it be!
Life from the dead is in that word;
　'Tis immortality.

2.

Here in the body pent,
　Absent from him I roam,
Yet nightly pitch my moving tent
　A day's march nearer home.

3.

My Father's house on high,
  Home of my soul, how near,
At times, to faith's far-seeing eye,
  Thy golden gates appear!

TRUST IN GOD.

HYMN 121. S. M.

FAR from my heavenly home,
  Far from my father's breast,
Fainting I cry, blest Spirit, come,
  And speed me to my rest.

2.

My spirit homeward turns,
  And fain would thither flee;
My heart, O Sion, droops and yearns,
  When I remember thee.

3.

To thee, to thee I press,
  A dark and toilsome road;
When shall I pass the wilderness,
  And reach the saints' abode?

4.

God of my life be near:
  On thee my hopes I cast:
O guide me through the desert here,
  And bring me home at last.

HYMN 122. L. M.

NO change of time shall ever shock
   My firm affection, Lord, to thee:
For thou hast always been my rock,
   A fortress and defense to me.

2.

Thou my deliverer art, my God;
   My trust is in thy mighty power:
Thou art my shield from foes abroad,
   At home my safeguard and my tower

3.

To thee I will address my prayer,
   To whom all praise we justly owe;
So shall I, by thy watchful care,
   Be guarded safe from every foe.

HYMN 123. L. M.

THY presence, Lord, hath me supplied,
   Thou my right hand support dost give;
Thou first shalt with thy counsel guide,
   And then to glory me receive.

2.

Whom then in heaven, but thee alone,
   Have I, whose favor I require?
Throughout the spacious earth there's none,
   Compared with thee, that I desire.

3.

My trembling flesh and aching heart
  May often fail to succor me;
But God shall inward strength impart,
  And my eternal portion be.

HYMN 124. 8s, 7s.

GOD shall charge his angel legions
  Watch and ward o'er thee to keep;
Though thou walk through hostile regions,
  Though in desert wilds thou sleep.

2.

On the lion, vainly roaring,
  On his young, thy foot shall tread;
And, the dragon's den exploring,
  Thou shalt bruise the serpent's head:

3.

Since, with pure and firm affection,
  Thou on God hast set thy love,
With the wings of his protection
  He will shield thee from above.

4.

Thou shalt call on him in trouble,
  He will hearken, he will save;
Here for grief reward thee double,
  Crown with life beyond the grave.

HYMN 125. 7s

LORD, for ever at thy side
  Let my place and portion be:

Strip me of the robe of pride,
  Clothe me with humility.

2.

Meekly may my soul receive
  All thy Spirit hath reveal'd:
Thou hast spoken, I believe,
  Though the oracle be seal'd.

3.

Humble as a little child,
  Weanèd from the mother's breast,
By no subtleties beguiled.
  On thy faithful word I rest.

4.

Israel! now and evermore
  In the Lord Jehovah trust;
Him, in all his ways, adore,
  Wise, and wonderful, and just.

HYMN 126. C. M.

WHO place on Sion's God their trust,
  Like Sion's rock shall stand;
Like her immovably be fix'd
  By his almighty hand.

2.

Look how the hills on every side
  Jerusalem enclose;
So stands the Lord around his saints,
  To guard them from their foes.

All those who walk in crooked paths,
  The Lord shall soon destroy;
Cut off th' unjust, but crown the saints
  With lasting peace and joy.

HYMN 127.   8s, 7s, 4s.

GUIDE me, O thou great Jehovah,
  Pilgrim through this barren land;
I am weak, but thou art mighty;
  Hold me with thy powerful hand:
    Bread of heaven,
  Feed me till I want no more.

2.

Open thou the crystal fountain,
  Whence the healing streams do flow;
Let the fiery, cloudy pillar
  Lead me all my journey through:
    Strong Deliverer,
  Be thou still my strength and shield.

3.

When I tread the verge of Jordan,
  Bid my anxious fears subside:
Death of death, and hell's destruction,
  Land me safe on Canaan's side;
    Songs of praises
  I will ever give to thee.

TRUST IN GOD.

HYMN 128. 7s.

'TIS my happiness below
  Not to live without the cross;
But the Saviour's power to know,
  Sanctifying every loss.

2.

Trials must and will befall;
  But with humble faith to see
Love inscribed upon them all—
  This is happiness to me.

3.

Did I meet no trials here,
  No chastisement by the way,
Might I not with reason fear
  I should be a castaway?

4.

Trials make the promise sweet;
  Trials give new life to prayer;
Bring me to my Saviour's feet,
  Lay me low, and keep me there.

HYMN 129. 10s.

THOUGH troubles assail, and dangers affright,
Though friends should all fail, and foes all unite,
Yet one thing secures us, whatever betide,
The promise assures us the Lord will provide.

2.

The birds without barn or storehouse are
    fed,
From them let us learn to trust for our
    bread;
His saints what is fitting shall ne'er be
    denied,
So long as 'tis written, The Lord will
    provide.

3.

His call we obey, like Abram of old,
We know not the way, but faith makes
    us bold;
For though we are strangers, we have a
    sure guide,
And trust in all dangers the Lord will
    provide.

4.

No strength of our own, nor goodness we
    claim,
Our trust is alone in Jesus's name;
In this, our strong tower, for safety we
    hide,
The Lord is our power, the Lord will
    provide.

5.

When life sinks apace, and death is in
    view,
The word of his grace shall comfort us
    through;

TRUST IN GOD.

Not fearing, or doubting; with Christ on
  our side,
We hope to die shouting, The Lord will
  provide.

HYMN 130. 8s.

THE Lord my pasture shall prepare,
  And feed me with a shepherd's care;
His presence shall my wants supply,
And guard me with a watchful eye;
My noonday walks he shall attend,
And all my midnight hours defend.

2.
When in the sultry glebe I faint,
Or on the thirsty mountain pant,
To fertile vales and dewy meads
My weary, wandering steps he leads,
Where peaceful rivers, soft and slow,
Amid the verdant landscape flow.

3.
Though in the paths of death I tread,
With gloomy horrors overspread,
My steadfast heart shall fear no ill,
For thou, O Lord, art with me still;
Thy friendly crook shall give me aid,
And guide me through the dreadful shade.

HYMN 131. C. M.

IN thee I put my steadfast trust,
  Defend me, Lord, from shame;

Incline thine ear, and save my soul,
  For righteous is thy name.

2.

Be thou my strong abiding place,
  To which I may resort:
Thy promise, Lord, is my defense,
  Thou art my rock and fort.

3.

My steadfast and unchanging hope
  Shall on thy power depend;
And I, in grateful songs of praise,
  My time to come will spend.

4.

While God vouchsafes me his support,
  I'll in his strength go on;
And other righteousness disclaim,
  And mention his alone.

5.

Therefore, with psaltery and harp,
  Thy truth, O Lord, I'll praise;
To thee, the God of Jacob's race,
  My voice in anthems raise.

HYMN 132. 12s.

WHEN through the torn sail the wild
    tempest is streaming,
When o'er the dark wave the red lightning is gleaming,

Nor hope lends a ray the poor seaman to cherish,
We fly to our Maker: "Save, Lord, or we perish."

2.

O Jesus, once rocked on the breast of the billow,
Aroused, by the shriek of despair, from thy pillow,
Now seated in glory, the mariner cherish,
Who cries in his anguish, "Save, Lord, or we perish."

3.

And O, when the whirlwind of passion is raging,
When sin in our hearts its wild warfare is waging,
Then send down thy Spirit thy redeemed to cherish,
Rebuke the destroyer: "Save, Lord, or we perish."

HYMN 133. P. M.

MY God, my Father, while I stray
Far from my home, on life's rough way,
O teach me from my heart to say,
  "Thy will be done."

2

Though dark my path, and sad my lot,
Let me be still and murmur not,

Or breathe the prayer divinely taught,
"Thy will be done."

3.
What though in lonely grief I sigh
For friends beloved no longer nigh,
Submissive still would I reply,
"Thy will be done."

4.
If thou shouldst call me to resign
What most I prize—it ne'er was mine;
I only yield thee what is thine—
"Thy will be done."

5.
Let but my fainting heart be blest
With thy sweet Spirit for its guest,
My God, to thee I leave the rest;
"Thy will be done."

6.
Renew my will from day to day,
Blend it with thine, and take away
All that now makes it hard to say,
"Thy will be done."

HYMN 134. C. M.

FATHER, whate'er of earthly bliss
 Thy sovereign will denies,
Accepted at thy throne of grace
 Let this petition rise.

2.
Give me a calm and thankful heart,
 From every murmur free;

TRUST IN GOD.

The blessings of thy grace impart,
 And let me live to thee.

3.

Let the sweet hope that thou art mine
 My path of life attend:
Thy presence through my journey shine,
 And crown my journey's end.

HYMN 135. 8s, 6s.

ALTHOUGH the vine its fruit deny,
 The budding fig tree droop and die,
  No oil the olive yield;
Yet will I trust me in my God,
Yea, bend rejoicing to his rod,
 And by his grace be heal'd.

2.

Though fields, in verdure once array'd,
By whirlwinds desolate be laid,
 Or parch'd by scorching beam;
Still in the Lord shall be my trust,
My joy; for though his frown is just,
 His mercy is supreme.

3.

Though from the folds the flock decay,
Though herds lie famish'd o'er the lea,
 And round the empty stall;
My soul above the wreck shall rise;
Its better joys are in the skies;
 There God is all in all.

1.

In God my strength, howe'er distress'd,
I yet will hope, and calmly rest,
  Nay, triumph in his love:
My lingering soul, my tardy feet,
Free as the hind he makes, and fleet,
  To speed my course above.

HYMN 136. 11s.

1.

HOW firm a foundation, ye saints of the Lord,
Is laid for your faith in his excellent word;
What more can he say than to you he hath said,
You who unto Jesus for refuge have fled:

2.

Fear not, I am with thee, O be not dismay'd,
I, I am thy God, and will still give thee aid;
I'll strengthen thee, help thee, and cause thee to stand,
Upheld by my righteous, omnipotent hand.

3.

When through the deep waters I call thee to go,
The rivers of woe shall not thee overflow;
For I will be with thee, thy troubles to bless,
And sanctify to thee thy deepest distress.

REDEMPTION.

4.

When through fiery trials thy pathway
    shall lie,
My grace, all sufficient, shall be thy sup-
    ply;
The flame shall not hurt thee, I only
    design
Thy dross to consume, and thy gold to
    refine.

5.

The soul that to Jesus hath fled for repose,
I will not, I will not desert to his foes;
That soul, though all hell shall endeavor
    to shake,
I'll never—no, never—no, never forsake.

REDEMPTION.

HYMN 137. C. M.

THERE is a fountain filled with blood,
    Drawn from Immanuel's veins;
And sinners plunged beneath that flood
    Lose all their guilty stains.

2.

The dying thief rejoiced to see
    That fountain in his day;
And there may I, as vile as he,
    Wash all my sins away.

3.

Dear dying Lamb, thy precious blood
  Shall never lose its power,
Till all the ransomed Church of God
  Be saved, to sin no more.

4.

E'er since, by faith, I saw the stream
  Thy flowing wounds supply,
Redeeming love has been my theme,
  And shall be till I die.

5.

Then in a nobler, sweeter song,
  I'll sing thy power to save,
When this poor, lisping, stammering tongue
  Lies silent in the grave.

HYMN 138. C. M.

THOU art the way, to thee alone
  From sin and death we flee;
And he who would the Father seek
  Must seek him, Lord, by thee.

2.

Thou art the Truth, thy truth alone
  True wisdom can impart;
Thou only canst inform the mind,
  And purify the heart.

3.

Thou art the Life, the rending tomb
  Proclaims thy conquering arm,

REDEMPTION.

And those who put their trust in thee
Nor death nor hell shall harm.

4.

Thou art the Way, the Truth, the Life;
  Grant us that way to know,
That truth to keep, that life to win,
  Whose joys eternal flow.

HYMN 139. C. M.

JESUS, the very thought of thee
  With sweetness fills the breast;
But sweeter far thy face to see,
  And in thy presence rest.

2.

No voice can sing, no heart can frame,
  Nor can the memory find
A sweeter sound than Jesus' name,
  The Saviour of mankind.

3.

O hope of every contrite heart,
  O joy of all the meek,
To those who fall, how kind thou art!
  How good to those who seek!

4.

But what to those who find? Ah! this
  Nor tongue nor pen can show;
The love of Jesus, what it is,
  None but his loved ones know.

5.

Jesus, our only joy be thou,
  As thou our prize wilt be;
In thee be all our glory now,
  And through eternity.

HYMN 140. C. M.

SALVATION! O the joyful sound!
  'Tis pleasure to our ears;
A sovereign balm for every wound,
  A cordial for our fears.

2.

Buried in sorrow and in sin,
  At hell's dark door we lay;
But we arise, by grace divine,
  To see a heavenly day.

3.

Salvation! let the echo fly
  The spacious earth around,
While all the armies of the sky
  Conspire to raise the sound.

4.

Salvation! O thou bleeding Lamb,
  To thee the praise belongs;
Salvation shall inspire our hearts,
  And dwell upon our tongues.

Chorus.

Glory, honor, praise, and power,
Be unto the Lamb for ever,
Jesus Christ is our Redeemer,
  Hallelujah, Amen.

REDEMPTION.

HYMN 141. 12s.

THE voice of free grace
  Cries, Escape to the mountain;
For Adam's lost race
  Christ hath opened a fountain:
For sin and uncleanness,
  And every transgression,
His blood flows most freely
  In streams of salvation.
    Hallelujah to the Lamb,
      Who hath bought us our pardon:
    We'll praise him again
      When we pass over Jordan.

2.

Ye souls that are wounded,
  To Jesus repair;
He calls you in mercy,
  And can you forbear?
Though your sins be as scarlet,
  Still flee to the mountain,
That blood can remove them
  Which streams from the fountain.
    Hallelujah, etc.

3.

O Jesus! ride onward,
  Triumphantly glorious:
O'er sin, death, and hell
  Thou art more than victorious:
Thy name is the theme
  Of the great congregation.

While angels and saints
 Raise the shout of salvation.
  Hallelujah, etc.

4.

With joy shall we stand
 When escaped to that shore;
With our harps in our hand
 We will praise him the more;
We'll range the sweet fields
 On the banks of the river,
And sing of salvation
 For ever and ever.
  Hallelujah, etc.

HYMN 142. 7s.

JESUS, lover of my soul,
 Let me to thy bosom fly,
While the billows near me roll,
 While the tempest still is high;
Hide me, O my Saviour, hide,
 Till the storm of life is past:
Safe into the haven guide;
 O receive my soul at last.

2.

Other refuge have I none,
 Hangs my helpless soul on thee,
Leave, O leave me not alone:
 Still support and comfort me.

REDEMPTION.

All my trust on thee is stayed;
  All my help from thee I bring;
Cover my defenseless head
  With the shadow of thy wing.

3.

Thou, O Christ, art all I want:
  Boundless love in thee I find:
Raise the fallen, cheer the faint,
  Heal the sick, and lead the blind.
Just and holy is thy name,
  I am all unrighteousness;
Vile, and full of sin I am,
  Thou art full of truth and grace.

4.

Plenteous grace with thee is found,
  Grace to pardon all my sin:
Let the healing streams abound:
  Make, and keep me pure within:
Thou of life the fountain art—
  Freely let me take of thee:
Spring thou up within my heart,
  Rise to all eternity!

HYMN 143. 7s.

ROCK of ages! cleft for me,
  Let me hide myself in thee:
Let the water and the blood,
From thy wounded side which flowed
Be of sin the double cure;
Save me from its guilt and power.

2.

Not the labor of my hands
Can fulfill thy law's demands;
Could my zeal no respite know;
Could my tears for ever flow;
All for sin could not atone;
Thou must save, and thou alone.

3.

Nothing in my hand I bring;
Simply to thy cross I cling:
Naked, come to thee for dress;
Helpless, look to thee for grace;
Vile, I to the fountain fly:
Wash me, Saviour, or I die!

4.

While I draw this fleeting breath,
When my eyelids close in death,
When I soar to worlds unknown,
See thee on thy judgment throne;
Rock of ages, cleft for me,
Let me hide myself in thee!

HYMN 144. L. M.

JESUS, thy blood and righteousness
My beauty are, my glorious dress,
Midst flaming worlds, in these array'd,
With joy shall I lift up my head.

2.

Bold shall I stand in thy great day,
For who aught to my charge shall lay?

REDEMPTION.

Fully absolved through these I am,
From sin and fear, and guilt and shame.

3.

When from the dust of death I rise
To claim my mansion in the skies,
E'en then this shall be all my plea—
Jesus hath lived, hath died for me.

4.

Thou God of power, thou God of love,
Let the whole world thy mercy prove;
Now let thy word o'er all prevail;
Now take the spoils of death and hell.

HYMN 145. C. M.

HOW sweet the name of Jesus sounds
In a believer's ear!
It soothes his sorrows, heals his wounds,
And drives away his fear.

2.

It makes the wounded spirit whole,
And calms the troubled breast;
'Tis manna to the hungry soul,
And to the weary rest.

3.

Dear name, the rock on which I build,
My shield and hiding place,
My never failing treasury, filled
With boundless stores of grace.

4.

Jesus! my Shepherd, Husband, Friend,
　My Prophet, Priest, and King, .
My Lord, my life, my way, my end—
　Accept the praise I bring.

THE CHURCH.
HYMN 146.　8s, 7s.

GLORIOUS things of thee are spoken,
　Sion, city of our God:
He whose word cannot be broken,
　Formed thee for his own abode;
On the rock of ages founded,
　What can shake thy sure repose?
With salvation's walls surrounded,
　Thou may'st smile at all thy foes.

2.

See the streams of living waters,
　Springing from eternal love,
Well supply thy sons and daughters,
　And all fear of want remove;
Who can faint while such a river
　Ever flows their thirst t'assuage?
Grace, which like the Lord, the Giver,
　Never fails from age to age.

3.

Round each habitation hovering,
　See the cloud and fire appear,
For a glory and a covering,
　Showing that the Lord is near.

THE CHURCH.

Blest inhabitants of Sion,
  Washed in the Redeemer's blood!
Jesus, whom their souls rely on,
  Makes them kings and priests to God.

4.

Saviour, if of Sion's city
  I through grace a member am,
Let the world deride or pity,
  I will glory in thy name:
Fading is the worldling's pleasure,
  All his boasted pomp and show;
Solid joys and lasting treasure,
  None but Sion's children know.

HYMN 147. L. M.

TRIUMPHANT Sion! lift thy head
  From dust, and darkness, and the dead:
Though humbled long, awake at length,
And gird thee with thy Saviour's strength.

2.

Put all thy beauteous garments on,
And let thy excellence be known:
Deck'd in the robes of righteousness,
The world thy glories shall confess.

3.

No more shall foes unclean invade,
And fill thy hallow'd walls with dread;
No more shall hell's insulting host
Their victory and thy sorrows boast.

HYMNS.

4.

God from on high has heard thy prayer,
His hand thy ruins shall repair:
Nor will thy watchful Monarch cease
To guard thee in eternal peace.

HYMN 148. S. M.

I LOVE thy kingdom, Lord,
   The house of thine abode,
The Church our blest Redeemer saved
   With his most precious blood.

2.

I love thy Church, O God;
   Her walls before thee stand,
Dear as the apple of thine eye,
   And graven on thy hand.

3.

If e'er to bless thy sons,
   My voice or hands deny,
These hands let useful skill forsake,
   This voice in silence die.

4.

If e'er my heart forget
   Her welfare, or her woe,
Let every joy this heart forsake,
   And every grief o'erflow.

5.

For her my tears shall fall;
   For her my prayers ascend;
To her my cares and toils be given,
   Till toils and cares shall end.

THE CHURCH.

6.
Beyond my highest joy
 I prize her heavenly ways,
Her sweet communion, solemn vows,
 Her hymns of love and praise.

7.
Jesus, thou Friend divine,
 Our Saviour and our King,
Thy hand from every snare and foe
 Shall great deliverance bring.

8.
Sure as thy truth shall last,
 To Sion shall be given,
The brightest glories earth can yield,
 And brighter bliss of heaven.

HYMN 149. C. M.

THE Lord, the only God, is great,
 And greatly to be praised
In Sion, on whose happy mount
 His sacred throne is raised.

2.
In Sion we have seen perform'd
 A work that was foretold,
In pledge that God, for times to come,
 His city will uphold.

3.
Let Sion's mount with joy resound;
 Her daughters all be taught
In songs his judgments to extol,
 Who this deliverance wrought.

4.

Compass her walls in solemn pomp,
   Your eyes quite round her cast;
Count all her towers, and see if there
   You find one stone displaced.

5.

Her forts and palaces survey,
   Observe their order well,
That to the ages yet to come
   His wonders you may tell.

6.

This God is ours, and will be ours,
   Whilst we in him confide;
Who, as he has preserved us now,
   Till death will be our guide.

HYMN 150. C. M.

O 'TWAS a joyful sound to hear
   Our tribes devoutly say,
Up, Israel, to the temple haste,
   And keep your festal-day!

2.

At Salem's courts we must appear,
   With our assembled powers,
In strong and beauteous order ranged
   Like her united towers.

3.

'Tis thither, by divine command,
   The tribes of God repair,
Before his ark to celebrate
   His Name with praise and prayer.

THE CHURCH.

4.

O, ever pray for Salem's peace;
 For they shall prosp'rous be,
Thou holy city of our God,
 Who bear true love to thee.

5.

May peace within thy sacred walls
 A constant guest be found;
With plenty and prosperity
 Thy palaces be crown'd.

6.

For my dear brethren's sake, and friends
 No less than brethren dear,
I'll pray—May peace in Salem's towers
 A constant guest appear.

HYMN 151. 8s, 7s.

CHILDREN of one common Father,
 Low before thy face we bow;
By the Holy Spirit gather
 Every heart to worship now;
Thou, in tenderness, art seeking
 Worship from thy children dear;
May our lips, thy love repeating,
 Yield the praise thou lov'st to hear.

2.

Abba, Father, we adore thee,
 Sweet paternal love is thine;
We delight to sing thy glory,
 And thy excellence divine;

HYMNS.

Thou hast loved us, still art loving,
  And thy love will never end;
Every earthly thought removing,
  Now let souls in worship blend.

3.

Hallelujah! Lord Almighty!
  God of grace, and truth, and love;
Praises, through thy Son, delight thee,
  Rising up to heaven above;
Perfumed by the holy incense
  Of his peerless, precious name,
While the Holy Spirit's presence
  Keeps alive the hallowed flame.

4.

Hallelujah! God and Father!
  Praise, adoring praise, be thine!
Praises now, and praise for ever,
  Praise exalted and divine!
Hallelujah! loud the chorus
  Shall resound o'er earth and sea!
Over death and hell victorious,
  Glory, glory, be to thee!

MISSIONS.

HYMN 152.   7s, 6s.

FROM Greenland's icy mountains,
  From India's coral strand,
Where Afric's sunny fountains
  Roll down their golden sand;

MISSIONS.

From many an ancient river,
  From many a palmy plain,
They call us to deliver
  Their land from error's chain.

2.

What though the spicy breezes
  Blow soft o'er Ceylon's isle;
Though every prospect pleases,
  And only man is vile:
In vain with lavish kindness
  The gifts of God are strewn;
The heathen in his blindness
  Bows down to wood and stone.

3.

Shall we, whose souls are lighted
  With wisdom from on high;
Shall we to men benighted
  The lamp of life deny?
Salvation, O salvation,
  The joyful sound proclaim,
Till each remotest nation
  Has learnt Messiah's name.

4.

Waft, waft, ye winds, his story,
  And you, ye waters, roll,
Till, like a sea of glory,
  It spreads from pole to pole:
Till o'er our ransom'd nature
  The Lamb for sinners slain,

Redeemer, King, Creator,
  In bliss returns to reign.

HYMN 153. L. M.

WHEN, Lord, to this our western land
    Led by thy providential hand,
  Our wandering fathers came,
Their ancient homes, their friends in
      youth,
Sent forth the heralds of thy truth,
  To keep them in thy name.

2.

Then, through our solitary coast,
The desert features soon were lost;
  Thy temples there arose;
Our shores, as culture made them fair,
Were hallowed by thy rites, by prayer,
  And blossomed as the rose.

3.

And O may we repay this debt
To regions solitary yet
  Within our spreading land;
There, brethren, from our common home,
Still westward, like our fathers, roam;
  Still guided by thy hand.

4.

Saviour, we own this debt of love:
O shed thy spirit from above,
  To move each Christian breast;

MISSIONS.

Till heralds shall thy truth proclaim,
And temples rise to fix thy name,
  Through all our desert west.

HYMN 154. L. M.

JESUS shall reign where'er the sun
  Does his successive journeys run;
His kingdom stretch from shore to shore,
Till moons shall wax and wane no more

2.
For him shall endless prayer be made,
And praises throng to crown his head;
His name like sweet perfume shall rise,
With every evening sacrifice.

3.
People and realms of every tongue
Dwell on his love with sweetest song,
And infant voices shall proclaim
Their early blessings on his name.

4.
Blessings abound where'er he reigns;
The prisoner leaps to lose his chains;
The weary find eternal rest;
And all the sons of want are blest.

5.
Let every creature rise and bring
Peculiar honors to our King;
Angels descend with songs again,
And earth repeat the loud Amen.

DEATH.

HYMN 155. S. M.

It is not death to die;
  To leave this weary road,
And 'midst the brotherhood on high
  To be at home with God.

2.

It is not death to close
  The eye long dimmed by tears,
And wake, in glorious repose,
  To spend eternal years.

3.

It is not death to bear
  The wrench that sets us free
From dungeon chain, to breathe the air
  Of boundless liberty.

4.

It is not death to fling
  Aside this sinful dust,
And rise, on strong, exulting wing,
  To live among the just.

5.

Jesus, thou Prince of life!
  Thy chosen cannot die;
Like thee, they conquer in the strife,
  To reign with thee on high.

DEATH.

HYMN 156. 11s.

I WOULD not live alway: I ask not to stay
Where storm after storm rises dark o'er
 the way;
The few lurid mornings that dawn on us
 here
Are enough for life's woes, full enough
 for its cheer.

2.

I would not live alway, thus fetter'd by
 sin,
Temptation without and corruption
 within:
E'en the rapture of pardon is mingled
 with fears,
And the cup of thanksgiving with penitent tears.

3.

I would not live alway; no, welcome the
 tomb:
Since Jesus hath lain there, I dread not
 its gloom;
There, sweet be my rest, till he bid me
 arise
To hail him in triumph descending the
 skies.

HYMN 157. 12s, 11s.

Thou art gone to the grave! but we will not deplore thee,
 Though sorrows and darkness encompass the tomb:
The Saviour has passed through its portal before thee,
 And the lamp of his love is thy guide through the gloom.

2.

Thou art gone to the grave! we no longer behold thee,
 Nor tread the rough path of the world by thy side;
But the wide arms of Mercy are spread to enfold thee,
 And sinners may hope, since the Sinless has died.

3.

Thou art gone to the grave! and, its mansion forsaking,
 Perhaps thy weak spirit in fear lingered long;
But the sunshine of Paradise beamed on thy waking,
 And the sound which thou heard'st was the seraphim's song.

DEATH.

4.

Thou art gone to the grave! but 'twere
    wrong to deplore thee,
For God was thy ransom, thy guardian,
    thy guide:
He gave thee, he took thee, and he will
    restore thee;
    And death has no sting, since the
    Saviour has died.

HYMN 158. L. M.

ASLEEP in Jesus! blessèd sleep!
From which none ever wake to weep;
A calm and undisturb'd repose,
Unbroken by the last of foes.

2.

Asleep in Jesus! O how sweet
To be for such a slumber meet:
With holy confidence to sing
That death hath lost its painful sting!

3.

Asleep in Jesus! peaceful rest,
Whose waking is supremely blest;
No fear, no woe shall dim that hour
That manifests the Saviour's power.

4.

Asleep in Jesus! O for me
May such a blissful refuge be!
Securely shall my ashes lie,
Waiting the summons from on high.

5.

Asleep in Jesus! far from thee
Thy kindred and their graves may be;
But there is still a blessèd sleep,
From which none ever wake to weep.

HYMN 159. C. M.

HEAR what the voice from heaven declares
  To those in Christ who die:
Released from all their earthly cares,
  They'll reign with him on high.

2.

Then why lament departed friends,
  Or shake at death's alarms?
Death's but the servant Jesus sends
  To call us to his arms.

3.

If sin be pardon'd, we're secure,
  Death hath no sting beside;
The law gave sin its strength and power,
  But Christ, our ransom, died.

4.

The grave of all his saints he bless'd,
  When in the grave he lay:
And, rising thence, their hopes he raised
  To everlasting day.

5.

Then, joyfully, while life we have,
  To Christ, our life, we'll sing,

Where is thy victory, O grave?
And where, O death, thy sting?

HYMN 160. S. M.

SERVANT of God, well done!
  Rest from thy loved employ;
The battle fought, the victory won,
  Enter thy Master's joy.

2.

At midnight came the cry,
  "To meet thy God prepare!"
He woke—and caught his Captain's eye;
  Strong both in faith and prayer.

3.

Tranquil amidst alarms,
  It found him in the field,
A veteran slumbering on his arms,
  Beneath his red-cross shield.

4.

His sword was in his hand,
  Still warm with recent fight,
Ready that moment, at command,
  Through rock and steel to smite.

5.

His spirit, with a bound,
  Left its encumbering clay;
His tent, at sunrise, on the ground,
  A darkened ruin lay.

HYMNS.

6.

The pains of death are past,
  Labor and sorrow cease;
And life's long warfare closed at last,
  His soul is found in peace.

7.

Soldier of Christ, well done!
  Praise be thy new employ;
And while eternal ages run,
  Rest in thy Saviour's joy.

MISCELLANEOUS.

HYMN 161. C. M.

ALL hail the power of Jesus' name!
  Let angels prostrate fall;
Bring forth the royal diadem,
  And crown him Lord of all.

2.

Ye chosen seed of Israel's race,
  Ye ransom'd from the fall,
Hail him who saves you by his grace,
  And crown him Lord of all.

3.

Hail him ye heirs of David's line,
  Whom David Lord did call,
The God incarnate! Man Divine!
  And crown him Lord of all.

4.

Sinners whose love can ne'er forget
　The wormwood and the gall;
Go, spread your trophies at his feet,
　And crown him Lord of all.

5.

Let every kindred, every tribe,
　On this terrestrial ball,
To him all majesty ascribe,
　And crown him Lord of all.

6.

Oh, that with yonder sacred throng
　We at his feet may fall;
We'll join the everlasting song,
　And crown him Lord of all.

HYMN 162.　8s, 7s.

GOD of mercy and compassion,
　Look with pity on my pain;
Hear a mournful broken spirit
　Prostrate at thy feet complain;
Many are my foes, and mighty;
　Strength to conquer I have none;
Nothing can uphold my goings,
　But thy blessed self alone.

2.

Saviour, look on thy beloved,
　Triumph over all my foes;
Turn to heavenly joy my mourning,
　Turn to gladness all my woes:

Live, or die, or work, or suffer,
　　Let my weary soul abide,
In all changes whatsoever,
　　Sure and steadfast by thy side.

3.

When temptations fierce assault me,
　　When my enemies I find,
Sin, and guilt, and death, and Satan,
　　All against my soul combined;
Hold me up in mighty waters,
　　Keep my eye on things above,
Righteousness, divine atonement,
　　Peace, and everlasting love!

HYMN 163. 7s.

HARK! the song of jubilee;
　　Loud as mighty thunders roar,
Or the fullness of the sea,
　　When it breaks upon the shore:
Hallelujah! for the Lord
　　God omnipotent shall reign;
Hallelujah! let the word
　　Echo round the earth and main.

2.

Hallelujah!—hark! the sound,
　　From the center to the skies,
Wakes above, beneath, around,
　　All creation's harmonies:
See Jehovah's banners furl'd;
　　Sheath'd his sword: he speaks, 'tis done,

And the kingdoms of this world
Are the kingdoms of his Son.

3.

He shall reign from pole to pole
  With illimitable sway;
He shall reign, when, like a scroll,
  Yonder heavens have pass'd away:
Then the end; beneath his rod,
  Man's last enemy shall fall;
Hallelujah! Christ in God,
  God in Christ, is all in all.

HYMN 164. 10s.

ABIDE with me: fast falls the eventide;
  The darkness deepens; Lord, with me abide:
When other helpers fail, and comforts flee,
Help of the helpless, O abide with me.

2.

Swift to its close ebbs out life's little day:
Earth's joys grow dim, its glories pass away;
Change and decay in all around I see;
O thou who changest not, abide with me.

3.

I need thy presence every passing hour;
What but thy grace can foil the tempter's power?

Who, like thyself, my guide and stay can
    be?
Through cloud and sunshine, Lord, abide
    with me.

4.

I fear no foe, with thee at hand to bless:
Ills have no weight, and tears no bitter-
    ness.
Where is death's sting? where, grave, thy
    victory?
I triumph still, if thou abide with me.

5.

Hold thou Thyself before my closing eyes;
Shine through the gloom, and point me to
    the skies;
Heaven's morning breaks, and earth's
    vain shadows flee;
In life, in death, O Lord, abide with me.

HYMN 165. C. M.

O THOU from whom all goodness flows,
    I lift my soul to thee;
In all my sorrows, conflicts, woes,
    O Lord! remember me.

2.

When on my aching, burdened heart,
    My sins lie heavily,
My pardon speak, new peace impart;
    In love remember me.

MISCELLANEOUS.

3.

Temptations sore obstruct my way,
  And ills I cannot flee,
O give me strength, Lord, as my day;
  For good remember me.

4.

If on my face, for thy dear name,
  Shame and reproach shall be,
I'll hail reproach, and welcome shame,
  If thou remember me.

5.

When in the solemn hour of death
  I wait thy just decree,
Saviour, with my last parting breath,
  I'll cry, Remember me.

HYMN 166. S. M.

IN mercy, not in wrath,
  Rebuke me, gracious God!
Lest, if thy whole displeasure rise,
  I sink beneath thy rod.

2.

Touch'd by thy quickening power,
  My load of guilt I feel;
The wounds thy Spirit hath unclosed,
  O let that Spirit heal.

3.

In trouble and in gloom,
  Must I for ever mourn?

And wilt thou not, at length, O God,
　In pitying love return?

4.

O come, ere life expire,
　Send down thy power to save;
For who shall sing thy Name in death,
　Or praise thee in the grave?

5.

Why should I doubt thy grace,
　Or yield to dread despair?
Thou wilt fulfill thy promised word,
　And grant me all my prayer.

HYMN 167.　L. P. M.

PEACE, troubled soul, whose plaintive moan
　Hath taught each scene the note of woe;
Cease thy complaint, suppress thy groan,
　And let thy tears forget to flow:
Behold, the precious balm is found,
　To lull thy pain and heal thy wound.

2.

Come, freely come, by sin opprest,
　On Jesus cast thy weighty load;
In him thy refuge find, thy rest,
　Safe in the mercy of thy God:
Thy God's thy Saviour, glorious word;
O hear, believe, and bless the Lord.

MISCELLANEOUS.

HYMN 168. C. M.

ON Jordan's stormy banks I stand,
   And cast a wishful eye
To Canaan's fair and happy land,
   Where my possessions lie.

2.

Oh, the transporting, rapturous scene,
   That rises to my sight!
Sweet fields arrayed in living green,
   And rivers of delight!

3.

O'er all those wide, extended plains,
   Shines one eternal day;
There God the Son forever reigns,
   And scatters night away.

4.

No chilling winds, nor poisonous breath,
   Can reach that healthful shore;
Sickness and sorrow, pain and death,
   Are felt and feared no more.

5.

When shall I reach that happy place,
   And be forever blest?
When shall I see my Father's face,
   And in his bosom rest?

6.

Filled with delight, my raptured soul
   Would here no longer stay;

Though Jordan's waves around me roll,
Fearless I'd launch away.

HYMN 169. 7s.

SINNERS! turn, why will ye die?
God, your Maker, asks you why:
God, who did your being give,
Made you with himself to live:
He the fatal cause demands,
Asks the work of his own hands;
Why, ye thankless creatures! why
Will ye cross his love, and die?

2.

Sinners! turn, why will ye die?
God, your Saviour, asks you why:
God, who did your souls retrieve,
That ye might for ever live;
Will you let him die in vain?
Crucify your Lord again?
Why, ye ransomed sinners, why
Will ye slight his grace, and die?

3.

Sinners! turn, why will ye die?
God, the Spirit, asks you why:
He who all your lives hath strove —
Wooed you to embrace his love.
Will ye not the grace receive?
Will ye still refuse to live?

Why, ye long-sought sinners, why
Will ye grieve your God, and die?

HYMN 170. C. M.

O RENDER thanks and bless the Lord,
   Invoke his sacred Name;
Acquaint the nations with his deeds,
   His matchless deeds proclaim.

2.

Sing to his praise in lofty hymns,
   His wondrous works rehearse;
Make them the theme of your discourse,
   And subject of your verse.

3.

Rejoice in his almighty Name,
   Alone to be adored;
And let their hearts o'erflow with joy,
   That humbly seek the Lord.

4.

Seek ye the Lord, his saving strength
   Devoutly still implore;
And, where he's ever present, seek
   His face for evermore.

5.

The wonders that his hands have wrought
   Keep thankfully in mind;
The righteous statutes of his mouth,
   And laws to us assign'd.

HYMN 171. C. M.

O FOR a closer walk with God,
  A calm and heavenly frame!
A light to shine upon the road
  That leads me to the Lamb!

2.

Where is the blessedness I knew,
  When first I saw the Lord?
Where is the soul-refreshing view
  Of Jesus and his word?

3.

What peaceful hours I once enjoyed;
  How sweet their memory still;
But they have left an aching void
  The world can never fill.

4.

Return, O holy Dove! return,
  Sweet messenger of rest!
I hate the sins that made thee mourn,
  And drove thee from my breast.

5.

The dearest idol I have known,
  Whate'er that idol be,
Help me to tear it from thy throne,
  And worship only thee.

6.

So shall my walk be close with God,
  Calm and serene my frame;
So purer light shall mark the road
  That leads me to the Lamb.

MISCELLANEOUS.

HYMN 172. L. M.

HE'S blest, whose sins have pardon gain'd,
   No more in judgment to appear;
Whose guilt remission has obtain'd,
   And whose repentance is sincere.

2.

No sooner I my wound disclosed,
   The guilt that tortured me within,
But thy forgiveness interposed,
   And mercy's healing balm pour'd in.

3.

Sorrows on sorrows multiplied
   The harden'd sinner shall confound;
But them who in His truth confide,
   Blessings of mercy shall surround.

4.

His saints, that have perform'd his laws,
   Their life in triumph shall employ;
Let them, as they alone have cause,
   In grateful raptures shout for joy.

HYMN 173. C. M.

AWAKE, my soul! stretch every nerve,
   And press with vigor on:
A heavenly race demands thy zeal,
   And an immortal crown.

2.

'Tis God's all-animating voice
  That calls thee from on high;
'Tis his own hand presents the prize
  To thine aspiring eye.

3.

A cloud of witnesses around
  Hold thee in full survey;
Forget the steps already trod,
  And onward urge thy way.

4.

Bless'd Saviour! introduced by thee,
  Have we our race begun;
And, crowned with victory, at thy feet
  We'll lay our laurels down.

HYMN 174. 7s.

SOFTLY now the light of day
  Fades upon my sight away;
Free from care, from labor free,
Lord, I would commune with thee:

2.

Thou, whose all-pervading eye
  Nought escapes, without, within,
Pardon each infirmity,
  Open fault, and secret sin.

3.

Soon, for me, the light of day
Shall for ever pass away;

Then, from sin and sorrow free,
Take me, Lord, to dwell with thee:

4.

Thou who, sinless, yet hast known
All of man's infirmity;
Then, from thine eternal throne,
Jesus, look with pitying eye.

HYMN 175. C. M.

GOD of our fathers, by whose hand
Thy people still are blest,
Be with us through our pilgrimage:
Conduct us to our rest.

2.

Through each perplexing path of life
Our wandering footsteps guide:
Give us each day our daily bread,
And raiment fit provide.

3.

O spread thy sheltering wings around,
Till all our wanderings cease,
And at our Father's loved abode
Our souls arrive in peace.

4.

Such blessings from thy gracious hand
Our humble prayers implore:
And thou, the Lord, shalt be our God,
And portion evermore.

HYMN 176. L. M.

JESUS, and shall it ever be,
A mortal man ashamed of thee?
Ashamed of thee, whom angels praise,
Whose glories shine thro' endless days?

2.

Ashamed of Jesus! sooner far
Let night disown each radiant star.
'Tis midnight with my soul, till he,
Bright Morning Star, bid darkness flee.

3.

Ashamed of Jesus! O, as soon
Let morning blush to own the sun;
He sheds the beams of light divine
O'er this benighted soul of mine.

4.

Ashamed of Jesus! that dear Friend
On whom my hopes of heaven depend!
No; when I blush, be this my shame,
That I no more revere his name.

5.

Ashamed of Jesus! empty pride;
I'll boast a Saviour crucified;
And, O, may this my portion be,
My Saviour not ashamed of me!

HYMN 177. 7s, 6s, 8s.

JESUS, let thy pitying eye
  Call back a wandering sheep;

False to thee, like Peter, I
  Would fain, like Peter, weep:
Let me be by grace restored,
  On me be all its freeness shown:
Turn and look upon me, Lord,
  And break my heart of stone.

2.

See me, Saviour, from above,
  Nor suffer me to die;
Life, and happiness, and love,
  Smile in thy gracious eye;
Speak the reconciling word,
  And let thy mercy melt me down;
Turn and look upon me, Lord,
  And break my heart of stone.

3.

Look, as when thy pitying eye
  Was closed, that we might live;
"Father," at the point to die,
  My Saviour gasped, "forgive!"
Surely with that dying word,
  He turns, and looks, and cries, "'Tis done!"
O my loving, bleeding Lord,
  This breaks my heart of stone.

HYMN 178. C. M.

THY chastening wrath, O Lord, restrain,
  Though I deserve it all;
Nor let on me the heavy storm
  Of thy displeasure fall.

2.

My sins, which to a deluge swell,
　My sinking head o'erflow,
And, for my feeble strength to bear,
　Too vast a burden grow.

3.

But, Lord, before thy searching eyes
　All my desires appear;
The groanings of my burden'd soul
　Have reach'd thine open ear.

4.

Forsake me not, O Lord, my God,
　Nor far from me depart:
Make haste to my relief, O thou
　Who my salvation art.

HYMN 179. C. M.

GOD moves in a mysterious way
　His wonders to perform;
He plants his footsteps in the sea,
　And rides upon the storm.

2.

Deep in unfathomable mines
　Of never-failing skill,
He treasures up his bright designs,
　And works his sovereign will.

3.

Ye fearful saints, fresh courage take;
　The clouds ye so much dread
Are big with mercy, and shall break
　In blessings on your head.

4.

Judge not the Lord by feeble sense,
  But trust him for his grace:
Behind a frowning providence
  He hides a smiling face.

5.

His purposes will ripen fast,
  Unfolding every hour;
The bud may have a bitter taste,
  But sweet will be the flower.

6.

Blind unbelief is sure to err,
  And scan his work in vain;
God is his own interpreter,
  And he will make it plain.

HYMN 180. L. M.

THOUGH I should seek to wash me clean
  In water of the driven snow,
My soul would yet its spot retain,
  And sink in conscious guilt and woe;

2.

The Spirit, in his power divine,
  Would cast my vaunting soul to earth,
Expose the foulness of its sin,
  And show the vileness of its worth.

3.

Ah, not like erring man is God,
  That men to answer him should dare;

Condemn'd, and into silence awed,
  They helpless stand before his bar.

4.

There, must a Mediator plead,
  Who God and man may both embrace:
With God, for man, to intercede,
  And give to man the purchased grace.

5.

And lo! the Son of God is slain
  To be this Mediator crowned:
In him, my soul, be cleansed from stain,
  In him thy righteousness be found!

HYMN 181. 8s, 7s.

SAVIOUR, breathe an evening blessing,
  Ere repose our spirits seal;
Sin and want we come confessing;
  Thou canst save and thou canst heal.
Though destruction walk around us,
  Though the arrow past us fly,
Angel-guards from thee surround us;
  We are safe if thou art nigh.

2.

Though the night be dark and dreary,
  Darkness cannot hide from thee;
Thou art He who, never weary,
  Watchest where thy people be.
Should swift death this night o'ertake us,
  And our couch become our tomb,
May the morn in heaven awake us,
  Clad in light and deathless bloom.

HYMN 182. 8s, 7s.

ONE there is, above all others,
   Well deserves the name of Friend;
His is love beyond a brother's,
   Costly, free, and knows no end:
They who once his kindness prove,
Find it everlasting love!

2.

Which, of all our friends, to save us,
   Could or would have shed their blood?
But our Jesus died to have us
   Reconciled in him to God:
This was boundless love indeed;
Jesus is a Friend in need.

3.

When he lived on earth abasèd,
   Friend of Sinners was his name;
Now, above all glory raisèd,
   He rejoices in the same:
Still he calls them brethren, friends,
And to all their wants attends.

4.

O for grace our hearts to soften!
   Teach us, Lord, at length to love;
We, alas! forget too often,
   What a Friend we have above;
But, when home our souls are brought,
We will love thee as we ought.

HYMN 183. L. M.

STAY, thou insulted Spirit, stay,
  Though I have done thee such despite:
Cast not a sinner quite away,
  Nor take thine everlasting flight.

2.

Though I have most unfaithful been,
  Of all who e'er thy grace received;
Ten thousand times thy goodness seen,
  Ten thousand times thy goodness grieved;

3.

Yet, O, the chief of sinners spare,
  In honor of my great High-priest;
Nor, in thy righteous anger, swear
  I shall not see thy people's rest.

4.

O Lord, my weary soul release,
  Upraise me by thy gracious hand;
Guide me into thy perfect peace,
  And bring me to the promised land.

HYMN 184. L. M.

HE'S blest, whose sins have pardon gain'd,
  No more in judgment to appear,
Whose guilt remission has obtain'd,
  And whose repentance is sincere.

2.

No sooner I my wound disclosed,
  The guilt that tortured me within,
But thy forgiveness interposed,
  And mercy's healing balm pour'd in.

3.

Sorrows on sorrows multiplied,
  The harden'd sinner shall confound;
But them who in his truth confide,
  Blessings of mercy shall surround.

4.

His saints that have perform'd his laws,
  Their life in triumph shall employ;
Let them, as they alone have cause,
  In grateful raptures shout for joy.

HYMN 185. C. M.

O HAPPY is the man who hears
  Religion's warning voice,
And who celestial wisdom makes
  His early, only choice.

2.

For she has treasures greater far
  Than east or west unfold;
More precious are her bright rewards
  Than gems, or stores of gold.

3.

Her right hand offers to the just
  Immortal, happy days;

Her left, imperishable wealth
   And heavenly crowns displays.

4.

And, as her holy labors rise,
   So her rewards increase;
Her ways are ways of pleasantness,
   And all her paths are peace.

HYMN 186. L. M.

LET me be with thee where thou art,
My Saviour, my eternal rest;
Then only will this longing heart
Be fully and for ever blest.

2.

Let me be with thee where thou art,
Thy unveiled glory to behold;
Then only will this wandering heart
Cease to be false to thee, and cold.

3.

Let me be with thee where thou art,
Where spotless saints thy name adore;
Then only will this sinful heart
Be evil and defiled no more.

4.

Let me be with thee where thou art,
Where none can die, where none remove;
There neither life nor death will part
Me from thy presence and thy love.

HYMN 187. 8s, 7s, 4s.

COME, ye sinners, poor and needy,
   Weak and wounded, sick and sore.
Jesus ready stands to save you,
   And his heart with love runs o'er:
     He is able,
  He is willing: doubt no more.

2.

Come, ye needy, come and welcome,
   God's free bounty glorify;
True belief and true repentance,
   Every grace that brings you nigh,
     Without money,
  Come to Jesus Christ and buy.

3.

Come, ye weary, heavy-laden,
   Lost and ruin'd by the fall,
If you tarry till you're better,
   You will never come at all:
     Not the righteous,
  Sinners Jesus came to call.

4.

Agonizing in the garden,
   Your Redeemer prostrate lies;
On the bloody tree behold him!
   Hear him cry, before he dies,
     "It is finish'd!"
  Sinners, will not this suffice?

5.

Lo! th' incarnate God, ascending,
　Pleads the merit of his blood;
Venture on him, venture wholly,
　Let no other trust intrude;
　　None but Jesus
　Can do helpless sinners good.

6.

Saints and angels, join'd in concert,
　Sing the praises of the Lamb;
While the blissful courts of heaven
　Sweetly echo with his name;
　　Hallelujah!
　Sinners here may sing the same.

HYMN 188.　C. M.

AS pants the hart for cooling streams,
　When heated in the chase;
So longs my soul, O God, for thee,
　And thy refreshing grace.

2.

For thee, my God, the living God,
　My thirsty soul doth pine;
O when shall I behold thy face,
　Thou Majesty divine?

3.

Why restless, why cast down, my soul?
　Trust God; who will employ
His aid for thee, and change these sighs
　To thankful hymns of joy.

4.
God of my strength, how long shall I
  Like one forgotten, mourn,
Forlorn, forsaken, and exposed
  To my oppressor's scorn?
5.
Why restless, why cast down, my soul?
  Hope still; and thou shalt sing
The praise of him who is thy God,
  Thy health's eternal spring.

HYMN 189. S. M.

A CHARGE to keep I have,
  A God to glorify;
A never-dying soul to save,
  And fit it for the sky:
2.
From youth to hoary age,
  My calling to fulfill:
O may it all my powers engage
  To do my Master's will.
3.
Arm me with jealous care,
  As in thy sight to live,
And O thy servant, Lord, prepare
  A strict account to give.
4.
Help me to watch and pray,
  And on thyself rely:
Assured if I my trust betray,
  I shall for ever die.

HYMN 190. S. M.

PART I.

HAVE mercy, Lord, on me,
　As thou wert ever kind;
Let me, oppress'd with loads of guilt,
　Thy wonted mercy find.

2.

Wash off my foul offense,
　And cleanse me from my sin;
For I confess my crime, and see
　How great my guilt has been.

3.

Against thee, Lord, alone,
　And only in thy sight,
Have I transgress'd; and, though condemn'd,
　Must own thy judgment right.

4.

In guilt each part was form'd
　Of all this sinful frame;
In guilt I was conceived, and born
　The heir of sin and shame.

PART II.

With hyssop purge me, Lord,
　And so I clean shall be:
I shall with snow in whiteness vie,
　When purified by thee.

2.

Make me to hear with joy
  Thy kind forgiving voice;
That so the bones which thou hast broke
  May with fresh strength rejoice.

3.

Blot out my crying sins,
  Nor me in anger view:
Create in me a heart that's clean,
  An upright mind renew.

4.

Withdraw not thou thy help,
  Nor cast me from thy sight;
Nor let thy Holy Spirit take
  His everlasting flight.

HYMN 191. L. M.

THE countless multitude on high,
  That tune their songs to Jesus' name,
All merit of their own deny,
  And Jesus' worth alone proclaim.

2.

Firm on the ground of sovereign grace,
  They stand before Jehovah's throne;
The only song in which blest place
  Is, "Thou art worthy! thou alone."

3.

While thus the ransom'd myriads shout,
  "Amen" the holy angels cry;
"Amen, Amen," resounds throughout
  The boundless regions of the sky.

4.

Let us with joy adopt the strain
    We hope to sing for ever there,
"Worthy's the Lamb for sinners slain;
    Worthy alone the crown to wear!"

5.

Without one thought that's good to plead,
    Oh! what could shield us from despair
But this, though we are vile indeed,
    The Lord our Righteousness is there.

HYMN 192. L. M.

SUN of my soul, thou Saviour dear,
It is not night if thou be near:
O may no earth-born cloud arise,
To hide thee from thy servant's eyes.

2.

When the soft dews of kindly sleep
My wearied eyelids gently steep,
Be my last thought, how sweet to rest
For ever on my Saviour's breast!

3.

Abide with me from morn till eve,
For without thee I cannot live:
Abide with me when night is nigh,
For without thee I dare not die.

4.

If some poor wandering child of thine
Have spurned, to-day, the voice divine,
Now, Lord, the gracious work begin;
Let him no more lie down in sin.

5.

Watch by the sick: enrich the poor
With blessings from thy boundless store.
Be every mourner's sleep, to-night,
Like infants' slumbers, pure and light.

6.

Come near and bless us when we wake,
Ere through the world our way we take:
Till in the ocean of thy love
We lose ourselves in heaven above.

HYMN 193. S. M.

My soul, be on thy guard;
    Ten thousand foes arise;
The hosts of sin are pressing hard
    To draw thee from the skies.

2.

O watch, and fight, and pray:
    The battle ne'er give o'er;
Renew it boldly every day,
    And help divine implore.

3.

Ne'er think the victory won,
    Nor lay thine armor down:
Thy arduous work will not be done
    Till thou obtain thy crown.

4.

Fight on, my soul, till death
    Shall bring thee to thy God:
He'll take thee, at thy parting breath,
    Up to his blest abode.

HYMN 194. S. M.

THE Spirit, in our hearts,
  Is whispering, Sinner, come:
The Bride, the Church of Christ, pro-
    claims
  To all his children, Come.

2.

Let him that heareth, say
  To all about him, Come:
Let him that thirsts for righteousness,
  To Christ, the fountain, come.

3.

Yes, whosoever will,
  O let him freely come,
And freely drink the stream of life:
  'Tis Jesus bids him come.

4.

Lo, Jesus, who invites,
  Declares, I quickly come.
Lord! even so; I wait thy hour:
  Jesus, my Saviour, come.

HYMN 195. C. M.

ALAS! and did my Saviour bleed?
  And did my Sovereign die?
Would he devote that sacred head
  For such a worm as I?

2.

Was it for crimes that I have done
  He groaned upon the tree?

Amazing pity! grace unknown!
  And love beyond degree!

3.

Well might the sun in darkness hide,
  And shut his glories in,
When God, the mighty Maker, died,
  For man, the creature's sin.

4.

Thus might I hide my blushing face,
  While his dear cross appears,
Dissolve my heart in thankfulness,
  And melt mine eyes in tears.

5.

But drops of grief can ne'er repay
  The debt of love I owe;
Here, Lord, I give myself away,
  'T is all that I can do.

HYMN 196. C. M.

THE Lord himself, the mighty Lord,
  Vouchsafes to be my guide;
The shepherd, by whose constant care
  My wants are all supplied.

2.

In tender grass he makes me feed,
  And gently there repose:
Then leads me to cool shades, and where
  Refreshing water flows.

3.

He does my wandering soul reclaim,
  And, to his endless praise,
Instruct with humble zeal to walk
  In his most righteous ways.

4.

I pass the gloomy vale of death
  From fear and danger free;
For there his aiding rod and staff
  Defend and comfort me.

5.

Since God doth thus his wondrous love
  Through all my life extend,
That life to him I will devote,
  And in his service spend.

HYMN 197. L. M.

O LORD, thy mercy, my sure hope,
  The highest orb of heaven transcends,
Thy sacred truth's unmeasured scope
  Beyond the spreading sky extends.

2.

Thy justice like the hills remains,
  Unfathom'd depths thy judgments are;
Thy providence the world sustains,
  The whole creation is thy care.

3.

Since of thy goodness all partake,
  With what assurance should the just
Thy sheltering wings their refuge make,
  And saints to thy protection trust!

4.

Such guests shall to thy courts be led,
 To banquet on thy love's repast;
And drink, as from a fountain's head,
 Of joys that shall for ever last.

5.

With thee the springs of life remain,
 Thy presence is eternal day;
O let thy saints thy favor gain,
 To upright hearts thy truth display.

HYMN 198. 7s.

SINNER, rouse thee from thy sleep,
Wake, and o'er thy folly weep;
Raise thy spirit, dark and dead,
Jesus waits his light to shed.

2.

Wake from sleep, arise from death,
See the bright and living path:
Watchful tread that path; be wise,
Leave thy folly, seek the skies.

3.

Leave thy folly, cease from crime,
From this hour redeem thy time;
Life secure without delay,
Evil is the mortal day.

4.

Be not blind and foolish still;
Called of Jesus, learn his will;
Jesus calls from death and night,
Jesus waits to shed his light.

HYMN 199. 7s.

HASTEN, sinner, to be wise:
  Stay not for the morrow's sun!
Wisdom, if you still despise,
  Harder is it to be won.

2.

Hasten mercy to implore;
  Stay not for the morrow's sun;
Lest thy season should be o'er,
  Ere this evening's stage be run.

3.

Hasten, sinner, to return;
  Stay not for the morrow's sun;
Lest thy lamp should cease to burn.
  Ere salvation's work is done.

4.

Hasten, sinner, to be blest;
  Stay not for the morrow's sun;
Lest perdition thee arrest,
  Ere the morrow is begun.

HYMN 200. H. M.

BLOW ye the trumpet, blow;
  The gladly solemn sound
Let all the nations know,
  To earth's remotest bound:
The year of jubilee is come,
Return, ye ransomed sinners, home.

2.

Jesus, our great High Priest,
  Has full atonement made;

Ye weary spirits, rest;
  Ye mourning souls, be glad:
The year of jubilee is come,
Return, ye ransomed sinners, home.

3.

Exalt the Lamb of God,
  The sin-atoning Lamb;
Redemption by his blood
    Through all the world proclaim:
The year of jubilee is come,
Return, ye ransomed sinners, home.

HYMN 201. S. M.

O WHERE shall rest be found,
  Rest for the weary soul?
'Twere vain the ocean's depths to sound,
  Or pierce to either pole.

2.

The world can never give
  The bliss for which we sigh:
'Tis not the whole of life to live,
  Nor all of death to die.

3.

Beyond this vale of tears
  There is a life above,
Unmeasured by the flight of years;
  And all that life is love.

4.

There is a death whose pang
  Outlasts the fleeting breath;

O what eternal horrors hang
Around the second death!

5.

Lord God of truth and grace,
  Teach us that death to shun,
Lest we be banished from thy face,
  And evermore undone.

HYMN 202. C. P. M.

JOIN'D in the bonds of faith and love,
  With saints on earth, and saints above,
    One spirit with our Lord,
In happy union here we meet,
To worship at the Saviour's feet,
    And own his work and word.

2.

Thy gracious promise, Lord, impart,
Display thy power in every heart,
    And shed thy blessing round.
Oh! may thy truth our spirits cheer,
Confirm our hope, dispel our fear,
    And make our joys abound.

HYMN 203. C. M.

I HEARD the voice of Jesus say,
  "Come unto me and rest;
Lay down, thou weary one, lay down
  Thy head upon my breast:"
I came to Jesus as I was,
  Weary, and worn, and sad;

I found in him a resting-place,
  And he has made me glad.

2.
I heard the voice of Jesus say,
  "Behold, I freely give
The living-water! thirsty one,
  Stoop down, and drink, and live.
I came to Jesus, and I drank
  Of that life-giving stream:
My thirst was quenched, my soul revived,
  And now I live in him.

3.
I heard the voice of Jesus say,
  "I am this dark world's light:
Look unto me: thy morn shall rise,
  And all thy day be bright."
I looked to Jesus, and I found
  In him my Star, my Sun;
And in that light of life I'll walk
  Till all my journey's done.

HYMN 204. P. M.

I LAY my sins on Jesus,
  The Spotless Lamb of God;
He bears them all and frees us
  From the accursed load:
I bring my guilt to Jesus,
  To wash my crimson stains
White in his blood most precious,
  Till not a stain remains.

2.

I lay my wants on Jesus;
  All fullness dwells in him;
He heals all my diseases,
  He doth my soul redeem:
I lay my griefs on Jesus,
  My burdens and my cares;
He from them all releases,
  He all my sorrow shares.

3.

I rest my soul on Jesus,
  This weary soul of mine;
His right hand me embraces,
  I on his breast recline.
I love the name of Jesus,
  Immanuel, Christ, the Lord;
Like fragrance on the breezes,
  His name abroad is poured.

HYMN 205.   L. M.

HARK, my soul, it is the Lord;
'Tis thy Saviour, hear his word;
Jesus speaks, he speaks to thee:
"Say, poor sinner, lov'st thou me?

2.

"I delivered thee when bound,
And when wounded heal'd thy wound,
Sought thee wandering, set thee right,
Turn'd thy darkness into light.

3.

"Can a woman's tender care
Cease toward the child she bare?
Yes, *she* may forgetful be,
Yet will *I* remember thee.

4.

"Mine is an unchanging love,
Higher than the heights above,
Deeper than the depths beneath,
Free and faithful, strong as death.

5.

"Thou shalt see my glory soon,
When the work of grace is done;
Partner of my throne shall be:
Say, poor sinner, lov'st thou me?"

6.

Lord, it is my chief complaint
That my love is still so faint,
Yet I love thee and adore:
O for grace to love thee more!

HYMN 206. H. M.

ARISE, my soul, arise;
  Shake off thy guilty fears;
The bleeding Sacrifice
  In my behalf appears:
Before the throne my Surety stands,
My name is written on his hands.

2.

He ever lives above,
  For me to intercede;

His all-redeeming love,
  His precious blood, to plead;
His blood atoned for all our race,
And sprinkles now the throne of grace.

3.

Five bleeding wounds he bears,
  Received on Calvary;
They pour effectual prayers,
  They strongly plead for me:
Forgive him, O forgive, they cry,
Nor let that ransom'd sinner die.

4.

My God is reconciled;
  His pard'ning voice I hear:
He owns me for his child;
  I can no longer fear:
With confidence I now draw nigh,
And Father, Abba, Father, cry.

HYMN 207. 7s.

DEPTH of mercy! can there be
  Mercy still reserved for me?
Can my God his wrath forbear?
Me, the chief of sinners, spare?

2.

I have long withstood his grace;
Long provoked him to his face;
Would not hearken to his calls;
Grieved him by a thousand falls.

3.

Kindled his relentings are;
Me he now delights to spare;

Now my Father's mercies move,
Justice lingers into love.

4.

Lo! for me the Saviour stands;
Shows his wounds, and spreads his hands;
God is love! I know, I feel;
Jesus weeps, and loves me still.

HYMN 208. 8s, 7.

JESUS, the Name high over all,
  In hell, or earth, or sky;
Angels and men before it fall,
  And devils fear and fly.

2.

Jesus, the Name to sinners dear,
  The Name to sinners given;
It scatters all their guilty fear;
  It turns their hell to heaven.

3.

Jesus the pris'ner's fetters breaks,
  And bruises Satan's head;
Power into strengthless souls he speaks,
  And life into the dead.

4.

O that the world might taste and see
  The riches of his grace;
The arms of love that compass me
  Would all mankind embrace.

5.

His only righteousness I show,
  His saving truth proclaim;

'Tis all my business here below
  To cry, Behold the Lamb!

6.

Happy, if with my latest breath
  I may but gasp his name;
Preach him to all, and cry in death,
  Behold, behold the Lamb!

HYMN 209. C. M.

MY God, the spring of all my joys,
  The life of my delights,
The glory of my brightest days,
  And comfort of my nights:

2.

In darkest shades if thou appear,
  My dawning is begun;
Thou art my soul's bright morning star,
  And thou my rising sun.

3.

The opening heavens around me shine
  With beams of sacred bliss,
If Jesus shows his mercy mine,
  And whispers I am his.

4.

My soul would leave this heavy clay
  At that transporting word,
Run up with joy the shining way,
  To see and praise my Lord.

5.

Fearless of hell and ghastly death,
I'd break through every foe;
The wings of love and arms of faith
Would bear me conqu'ror through

HYMN 210. L. M.

JUST as thou art, without one trace
Of love, or joy, or inward grace,
Or meetness for that heavenly place,
O guilty sinner, come, O come!

2.

Thy sins I bore on Calvary's tree;
The stripes thy due were laid on me,
That peace and pardon might be free;
O wretched sinner, come, O come!

3.

Come, leave thy burden at the cross:
Count all thy gains but empty dross:
My grace repays all earthly loss;
O needy sinner, come, O come!

4.

"The Spirit and the Bride say, Come:"
Rejoicing saints re-echo, Come!
Who faints, who thirsts, who will, may come;
Thy Saviour bids thee come, O come!

HYMN 211. C. M.

HOW sweet a voice of sov'reign grace
Sounds from the sacred word!

Ho! ye despairing sinners, come,
   And trust a faithful Lord.

2.

My soul obeys the gracious call,
   And runs to this relief;
I would believe thy promise, Lord;
   O help my unbelief!

3.

To the blest fountain of thy blood,
   Incarnate God, I fly;
Here let me wash my guilty soul
   From crimes of deepest dye.

4.

A guilty, weak, and helpless worm,
   Into thine arms I fall;
Be thou my strength and righteousness,
   My Jesus, and my all.

HYMN 212. S. M.

I WAS a wand'ring sheep,
   I did not love the fold;
I did not love my Shepherd's voice,
   I would not be controll'd;
I was a wayward child,
   I did not love my home;
I did not love my Father's voice,
   I loved afar to roam.

2

The Shepherd sought his sheep,
   The Father sought his child;

They follow'd me o'er vale and hill,
　O'er deserts, waste and wild;
They found me nigh to death,
　Famish'd, and faint, and lone;
They bound me with the bands of love,
　They saved the wand'ring one.

3.

Jesus my Shepherd is,
　'T was he that loved my soul;
'T was He that wash'd me in his blood,
　'T was he that made me whole;
No more a wand'ring sheep,
　I love to be controll'd;
I love my tender Shepherd's voice,
　I love the peaceful fold.

HYMN 213. P. M.

COME, ye disconsolate, where'er ye languish;
　Come to the mercy-seat, fervently kneel;
Here bring your wounded hearts, here tell your anguish;
　Earth has no sorrow that Heaven cannot heal.

2.

Joy of the desolate, light of the straying,
　Hope of the penitent, fadeless and pure.

Here speaks the Comforter, tenderly say-
ing,
Earth has no sorrow that Heaven cannot cure.

3.

Here see the bread of life; see waters
flowing
Forth from the throne of God, pure
from above:
Come to the feast of love; come, ever
knowing,
Earth has no sorrow but Heaven can
remove.

HYMN 214. L. M.

JESUS, thou everlasting King,
Accept the tribute which we bring;
Accept thy well-deserved renown,
And wear our praises as thy crown.

2.

Let every act of worship be
Like our espousals, Lord, to thee;
Like the blest hour, when from above
We first received the pledge of love.

3.

The gladness of that happy day,
O may it ever, ever stay:
Nor let our faith forsake its hold,
Nor hope decline, nor love grow cold.

4.

Let every moment, as it flies,
Increase thy praise, improve our joys,
Till we be raised to sing thy Name,
At the great supper of the Lamb.

HYMN 215. P. M.

PART I.

JESUS, I my cross have taken,
  All to leave and follow thee,
Naked, poor, despised, forsaken,
  Thou, from hence, my all shalt be.
Perish every fond ambition,
  All I've sought, or hoped, or known,
Yet how rich is my condition,
  God and heaven are all my own.

2.

Let the world despise and leave me;
  They have left my Saviour too;
Human hopes and looks deceive me,
  Thou art not like them, untrue;
And while thou shalt smile upon me,
  God of wisdom, love, and might,
Foes may hate, and friends may scorn me,
  Show thy face and all is bright.

3.

Go, then, earthly fame and treasure;
  Come disaster, scorn, and pain;
In thy service pain is pleasure;
  With thy favor loss is gain.

HYMNS.

I have called thee Abba, Father;
  I have set my heart on thee;
Storms may howl, and clouds may gather:
  All must work for good to me.

PART I4.

Man may trouble and distress me,
  'T will but drive me to thy breast;
Life with trials hard may press me,
  Thou canst give me sweetest rest.
O, 'tis not in grief to harm me,
  While thy love is left to me;
O, 'twere not in joy to charm me,
  Were that joy unmixed with thee !

2.

Know, my soul, thy full salvation;
  Rise o'er sin and fear and care;
Joy to find, in every station,
  Something still to do and bear.
Think what Spirit dwells within thee,
  Think what Father's smiles are thine,
Think that Jesus died to win thee;
  Child of heaven, canst thou repine?

3.

Haste thee on from grace to glory,
  Arm'd by faith, and wing'd by prayer;
Heaven's eternal days before thee,
  God's own hand shall guide thee there;
Soon shall close thine earthly mission,
  Soon shall pass thy pilgrim days:

Hope shall change to glad fruition,
  Faith to sight, and prayer to praise.

HYMN 216. S. M.

ONE sweetly solemn thought
  Comes to me o'er and o'er;
I'm nearer to my home to-day
  Than e'er I've been before:

2.

Nearer my Father's house,
  Where many mansions be;
Nearer the great encircled throne,
  Nearer the crystal sea;

3.

Nearer the bound of life,
  Where burdens are laid down;
Nearer resigning every cross,
  Nearer the starry crown:

4.

But waves of death's still sea
  Roll dark before my sight,
That brightly on the other side
  Break on a shore of light.

5.

O, if my mortal feet
  Have almost gained the brink,
If it be I am nearer home
  Much nearer than I think:

6.

Father, perfect my trust,
That I may feel, in death,
My soul her feet hath firmly set
On Christ, the Rock of faith!

HYMN 217. P. M.

WHEN this passing world is done,
When has sunk yon glowing sun,
When we stand with Christ in glory,
Looking o'er life's finished story,
Then, Lord, shall I fully know,
Not till then, how much I owe.

2.

When I stand before the throne,
Dressed in beauty not my own,
When I see thee as thou art,
Love thee with unsinning heart,
Then, Lord, shall I fully know,
Not till then, how much I owe.

3.

When the praise of heaven I hear,
Loud as thunder to the ear,
Loud as many waters' noise,
Sweet as harp's melodious voice,
Then, Lord, shall I fully know,
Not till then, how much I owe.

HYMN 218. C. M.

GREAT God, with wonder and with praise
On all thy works I look;

MISCELLANEOUS.

But still thy wisdom, power, and grace,
  Shine brightest in thy book.

2.

The stars that in their courses roll,
  Have much instruction given;
But thy good word informs my soul
  How I may soar to heaven.

3.

The fields provide my food, and show
  The goodness of the Lord;
But fruits of life and glory grow
  In thy most holy word.

4.

Here are my choicest treasures hid,
  Here my best comfort lies;
Here my desires are satisfied,
  And here my hopes arise.

5

Lord, make me understand thy law,
  Show what my faults have been;
And from thy Gospel let me draw
  Pardon for all my sin.

6.

Here would I learn how Christ has died
  To save my soul from hell;
Not all the books on earth beside,
  Such heavenly wonders tell.

7.

Than let me love my Bible more,
  And take a fresh delight,

By day to read these wonders o'er,
 And meditate by night.

HYMN 219. L. M.

JESUS, where'er thy people meet,
 There they behold thy mercy-seat;
Where'er they seek thee, thou art found,
And every place is hallowed ground.

2.

For thou, within no walls confined,
Inhabitest the humble mind;
Such ever bring thee where they come,
And going, take thee to their home.

3.

Dear Shepherd of thy chosen few,
Thy former mercies here renew;
Here to our waiting hearts proclaim
The sweetness of thy saving Name.

4.

Here may we prove the power of prayer
To strengthen faith, and sweeten care,
To teach our faint desires to rise,
And bring all heaven before our eyes.

HYMN 220. P. M.

WHEN gathering clouds around I view,
 And days are dark, and friends are few,
On him I lean, who, not in vain,
Experienced every human pain;

He feels my griefs, he sees my fears,
And counts and treasures up my tears.

2.

If aught should tempt my soul to stray
From heavenly wisdom's narrow way,
To fly the good I would pursue,
Or do the ill I would not do;
Still he who felt temptation's power
Shall guard me in that dangerous hour.

3.

When vexing thoughts within me rise,
And, sore dismayed, my spirit dies;
Then he who once vouchsafed to bear
The midnight agony of prayer,
Shall sweetly soothe, shall gently dry,
The throbbing heart, the streaming eye.

4.

When sorrowing o'er some stone I bend,
Which covers all that was a friend,
And from his voice, his hand, his smile,
Divides me for a little while;
Thou, Saviour, seest the tears I shed,
For thou didst weep o'er Lazarus dead.

5.

And, oh, when I have safely past
Through every conflict but the last,
Still, still unchanging, watch beside
My bed of death, for thou hast died:
Then point to realms of endless day,
And wipe the latest tear away

HYMN 221. S. M.

GRACE! 'tis a charming sound,
   Harmonious to the ear;
Heaven with the echo shall resound,
   And all the earth shall hear.

2.

Grace first contrived a way
   To save rebellious man,
And all the means that grace display,
   Which drew the wondrous plan.

3.

Grace guides my wandering feet
   To tread the heavenly road;
And new supplies each hour I meet
   While pressing on to God.

4.

Grace all the work shall crown
   Through everlasting days;
It lays in heaven the topmost stone,
   And well deserves the praise.

HYMN 222. 7s.

SEEK, my soul, the narrow gate,
Enter ere it be too late;
Many ask to enter there
When too late to offer prayer.

2.

God from mercy's seat shall rise,
And for ever bar the skies:

Then, though sinners cry without,
He will say, "I know you not."

3.

Mournfully will they exclaim:
"Lord, we have professed thy name;
We have ate with thee, and heard
Heavenly teaching in thy word."

4.

Vain, alas, will be their plea,
Workers of iniquity;
Sad their everlasting lot;
Christ will say, "I know you not."

HYMN 223. 8s, 6s.

AWAKED by Sinai's awful sound,
My soul in bonds of guilt I found,
  And knew not where to go;
Eternal truth did loud proclaim,
"The sinner must be born again,
  Or sink to endless woe."

2.

When to the law I trembling fled,
It poured its curses on my head,
  I no relief could find;
This fearful truth increased my pain,
"The sinner must be born again,"
  And whelmed my tortured mind.

3.

Again did Sinai's thunder roll,
And guilt lay heavy on my soul,
  A vast oppressive load;
Alas, I read and saw it plain,
"The sinner must be born again,
  Or drink the wrath of God."

4.

The saints I heard with rapture tell,
How Jesus conquered death and hell,
  And broke the fowler's snare:
Yet when I found this truth remain,
"The sinner must be born again,"
  I sunk in deep despair.

5.

But while I thus in anguish lay,
The gracious Saviour passed this way,
  And felt his pity move;
The sinner, by his justice slain,
Now by his grace is born again,
  And sings redeeming love.

HYMN 224. L. M.

FAR from my thoughts, vain world,
  begone:
Let my religious hours alone:
From flesh and sense I would be free,
And hold communion, Lord, with thee.

2.

My heart grows warm with holy fire,
And kindles with a pure desire

To see thy grace, to taste thy love,
And feel thine influence from above.

3.

When I can say that God is mine,
When I can see thy glories shine,
I'll tread the world beneath my feet,
And all that men call rich and great.

4.

Send comfort down from thy right hand,
To cheer me in this barren land;
And in thy worship let me know
The joys that from thy presence flow.

HYMN 225. 7s.

LORD, my God, I long to know,
  Oft it causes anxious thought,
Do I love thee, Lord, or no?
  Am I thine, or am I not?

2.

Could my heart so hard remain,
  Prayer a task and burden prove,
Any duty give me pain,
  If I knew a Saviour's love?

3.

When I turn mine eyes within,
  O how dark, and vain, and wild!
Prone to unbelief and sin,
  Can I deem myself thy child?

HYMNS.

4.

Yet I mourn my stubborn will,
  Find my sin a grief and thrall:
Should I grieve for what I feel,
  If I did not love at all?

5.

Could I love thy saints to meet,
  Choose the ways I once abhorr'd,
Find at times the promise sweet,
  If I did not love thee, Lord?

6.

Saviour, let me love thee more,
  If I love at all, I pray;
If I have not loved before,
  Help me to begin to-day.

HYMN 226. L. M.

BE still, my heart, these anxious cares
  To thee are burdens, thorns, and snares;
They cast dishonor on thy Lord,
And contradict his gracious word.

2.

Brought safely by his hand thus far,
Why wilt thou now give place to fear?
How canst thou want if he provide,
Or lose thy way with such a guide?

3.
When first before his mercy-seat
Thou didst to him thy all commit;
He gave thee warrant, from that hour,
To trust his wisdom, love, and power.

4.
Did ever trouble yet befall,
And he refuse to hear thy call?
And has he not his promise past,
That thou shalt overcome at last?

5.
Though rough and thorny be the road,
It leads thee home, apace to God;
Then count thy present trials small,
For heaven will make amends for all.

HYMN 227. L. M.

FAITH is the Christian's evidence
  Of things unseen by mortal eye;
It passes all the bounds of sense,
  And penetrates the inmost sky.

2.
Things absent it can set in view,
  And bring far distant prospects home:
Events long past it can renew,
  And long foresee the things to come.

3.
With strong persuasion, from afar
  The heavenly region it surveys,
Embraces all the blessings there,
  And here enjoys the promises.

4.

By faith a steady course we steer,
  Through ruffling storms and swelling seas,
O'ercome the world, keep down our fear,
  And still possess our souls in peace.

5.

By faith we pass the vale of tears,
  Safe and serene, though oft distress'd;
By faith, subdue the king of fears,
  And go rejoicing to our rest.

HYMN 228. C. M.

SEE, in the vineyard of the Lord,
  A barren fig-tree stands;
No fruit it yields, no blossom bears,
  Though planted by his hands.

2.

From year to year the tree he views,
  And still no fruit is found:
Then "cut it down," the Lord commands,
  "Why cumbers it the ground?"

3.

But lo! the gracious Saviour pleads,
  "The barren fig-tree spare,
Another year in mercy wait,
  It yet may bloom and bear:

4.

"But if my culture prove in vain,
  And still no fruit be found,

MISCELLANEOUS.

I plead no more; destroy the tree,
  And root it from thy ground."

HYMN 229. C. M.

THE head that once was crown'd with thorns,
  Is crown'd with glory now;
A royal diadem adorns
  The mighty Victor's brow.

2.
The highest place that heaven affords,
  Is to our Jesus given;
The King of kings, and Lord of lords,
  He reigns o'er earth and heaven.

3.
The joy of all who dwell above,
  The joy of all below,
To whom he manifests his love,
  And grants his name to know.

4.
To them the cross, with all its shame,
  With all its grace, is given;
Their name, an everlasting name.
  Their joy, the joy of heaven.

5.
They suffer with their Lord below,
  They reign with him above;
Their everlasting joy to know
  The myst'ry of his love.

HYMN 230.   8s, 7s, 4s.

LORD, dismiss us with thy blessing,
  Fill our hearts with joy and peace;
Let us each, thy love possessing,
  Triumph in redeeming grace:
    O refresh us,
  Traveling through this wilderness.

2.

Thanks we give, and adoration,
  For thy gospel's joyful sound;
May the fruits of thy salvation
  In our hearts and lives abound!
    Ever faithful
  To the truth may we be found.

3.

So whene'er the signal's given,
  Us from earth to call away,
Borne on angels' wings to heaven,
  Glad the summons to obey,
    May we ever
  Reign with Christ in endless day.

DOXOLOGY.   L. M.

PRAISE God from whom all blessings
    flow;
Praise him all creatures here below;
Praise him above, ye heavenly host;
Praise Father, Son, and Holy Ghost.
                          Amen.

INDEX OF HYMNS.

	HYMN
A charge to keep I have	189
A glory gilds the sacred page	109
Abide with me: fast falls the eventide	164
Alas! and did my Saviour bleed	195
All hail the power of Jesus' name	161
Although the vine its fruit deny	135
And are we now brought near to God	49
Angels from the realms of glory	7
Another six days' work is done	97
Approach, my soul, the mercy-seat	88
Arise, my soul arise	206
Asleep in Jesus! blessed sleep	158
As o'er the past my memory strays	102
As pants the hart for cooling streams	188
Awake, my soul! stretch every nerve	173
Awake, my soul, to joyful lays	72
Awake, ye saints, awake	98
Awaked by Sinai's awful sound	223
Before Jehovah's awful throne	70
Behold the Saviour of mankind	26
Be still, my heart, these anxious cares	226
Blest be the tie that binds	103
Blow ye the trumpet, blow	200
Bread of the world, in mercy broken	50
Brightest and best of the sons of the morning	14

INDEX OF HYMNS.

	HYMN
Calm on the listening ear of night	10
Children of the heavenly King	69
Children of one common Father	151
Christ the Lord is risen to day	32
Come, Holy Spirit, come	38
Come, Holy Spirit, Heavenly Dove	36
Come, let us join our friends above	104
Come, thou Fount of every blessing	80
Come ye disconsolate, where'er ye languish	213
Come, ye sinners, poor and needy	187
Come, ye that love the Lord	76
Depth of mercy! can there be	207
Faith is the Christian's evidence	227
Far from my heavenly home	121
Far from my thoughts, vain world, begone	224
Father of all, whose love profound	40
Father of mercies, bow thine ear	57
Father of mercies! in thy word	107
Father, whate'er of earthly bliss	134
For ever here my rest shall be	30
For ever with the Lord	120
For thee, O dear, dear Country	115
From all that dwell below the skies	78
From every stormy wind that blows	84
From Greenland's icy mountains	152
Glorious things of thee are spoken	146
Glory to thee, my God, this night	75
God bless our native land	43
God moves in a mysterious way	179
God, my King, thy might confessing	71
God of mercy and compassion	162

INDEX OF HYMNS.

	HYMN
God of our fathers, by whose hand	175
God shall charge his angel legions	124
God's perfect law converts the soul	108
Go forth, ye heralds, in my Name	58
Go, speak of Jesus! of that love	59
Grace! 'tis a charming sound	221
Great God, to thee my evening song	73
Great God, with wonder and with praise	218
Guide me, O thou great Jehovah	127
Hail! thou long expected Jesus	2
Hail, thou once despisèd Jesus	28
Hail to the Lord's Anointed	13
Happy the man that finds the grace	92
Hark! hark, my soul	114
Hark! my soul, it is the Lord	205
Hark! the glad sound, the Saviour comes	1
Hark! the herald angels sing	5
Hark! the song of jubilee	163
Hark! what mean those holy voices	11
Hasten, sinner, to be wise	199
Have mercy, Lord, on me	190
Hear what the voice from heaven declares	159
He's blest, whose sins have pardon gain'd	172
He's come, let every knee be bent	37
Holy Father, great Creator	41
How beauteous are their feet	15
How firm a foundation, ye saints of the Lord	136
How oft, alas! this wretched heart	19
How sweet the name of Jesus sounds	145
How sweet a voice of sov'reign grace	211
I heard the voice of Jesus say	203
I lay my sins on Jesus	204

INDEX OF HYMNS.

	HYMN
I was a wandering sheep	212
I love thy kingdom, Lord	148
I would not live alway; I ask not to stay	156
In mercy, not in wrath	166
Inspirer and hearer of prayer	85
In thy name, O Lord, assembling	91
In thee I put my steadfast trust	131
It is not death to die	155
Jehovah reigns, let all the earth	65
Jerusalem, my happy home	119
Jerusalem the golden	116
Jesus, and shall it ever be	176
Jesus, I my cross have taken	215
Jesus, let thy pitying eye	177
Jesus, lover of my soul	142
Jesus, my strength, my hope	89
Jesus! Name of wondrous love	9
Jesus shall reign where'er the sun	154
Jesus, the Name high over all	208
Jesus, the very thought of thee	139
Jesus, thou everlasting King	214
Jesus, thy blood and righteousness	144
Jesus, where'er thy people meet	219
Join'd in the bonds of faith and love	202
Joy to the world! the Lord is come	3
Just as I am, without one plea	56
Just as thou art, without one trace	210
Let me be with thee where thou art	186
Lo, he comes, with clouds descending	4
Lord, dismiss us with thy blessing	230
Lord, for ever at thy side	125
Lord! in the morning thou shalt hear	95

INDEX OF HYMNS.

	HYMN
Lord, my God, I long to know................	225
Lord, with glowing heart I'd praise thee.....	74
Lo! what a cloud of witnesses................	105
Magnify Jehovah's Name.................	63
'Mid scenes of confusion and creature complaints...	113
My faith looks up to thee.......................	54
My God, and is thy table spread.............	48
My God, how endless is thy love.............	79
My God, my Father, while I stray............	133
My God, permit me not to be.................	22
My God, the spring of all my joys............	209
My soul, be on thy guard......................	193
Nearer, my God, to thee.......................	23
No change of time shall ever shock..........	122
Not to the terrors of the Lord.................	106
O bless the Lord, my soul.....................	83
O come, loud anthems let us sing...........	68
O for a closer walk with God.................	171
O for a heart to praise my God...............	62
O for a thousand tongues to sing............	64
O God of hosts, the mighty Lord.............	96
O God, our help in ages past.................	99
O gracious God, in whom I live..............	24
O happy is the man who hears...............	185
O Holy, holy, holy Lord........................	39
O Lord, thy mercy, my sure hope...........	197
O Mother dear, Jerusalem....................	117
O render thanks and bless the Lord.........	170
O render thanks to God above...............	61

INDEX OF HYMNS.

	HYMN
O Spirit of the living God	60
O that my load of sin were gone	20
O Thou from whom all goodness flows	165
O Thou to whose all-searching sight	21
O 'twas a joyful sound to hear	150
O where shall rest be found	201
Oft in danger, oft in woe	55
On Jordan's stormy banks I stand	168
One sweetly solemn thought	216
One there is, above all others	182
Our Lord is risen from the dead	33
Peace, troubled soul, whose plaintive moan	167
Praise to God, immortal praise	42
Prayer is the soul's sincere desire	87
Rejoice, the Lord is King	35
Rise, crown'd with light, imperial Salem, rise	12
Rise, my soul, and stretch thy wings	111
Rock of ages! cleft for me	143
Salvation! O the joyful sound	140
Saviour, breathe an evening blessing	181
Saviour, like a shepherd lead us	45
Saviour, when in dust to thee	18
Saviour, who thy flock art feeding	44
See, in the vineyard of the Lord	228
Seek, my soul, the narrow gate	222
Servant of God, well done	160
Shout the glad tidings, exultingly sing	6
Sinner, rouse thee from thy sleep	198
Sinners! turn, why will ye die	169
Softly now the light of day	174
Soldiers of Christ, arise	46

INDEX OF HYMNS.

	HYMN
Songs of praise the angels sang	67
Stay, thou insulted Spirit, stay	183
Sun of my soul, thou Saviour dear	192
Sweet is the work, my God, my King	66
Sweet the moments, rich in blessing	29
The countless multitude on high	191
The God of life, whose constant care	100
The head that once was crown'd with thorns	229
The Lord himself, the mighty Lord	196
The Lord my pasture shall prepare	130
The Lord, the only God, is great	149
The Spirit, in our hearts	194
The voice of free grace	141
There is a fountain filled with blood	137
There is a land of pure delight	110
Thine for ever: God of love	53
This is the day of light	90
Thou art gone to the grave! but we will not deplore thee	157
Thou art the way, to thee alone	138
Thou, God, all glory, honor, power	51
Though I should seek to wash me clean	180
Though troubles assail and dangers affright	129
Through all the changing scenes of life	81
Thy chastening wrath, O Lord, restrain	178
Thy presence, Lord, hath me supplied	123
'Tis finished: so the Saviour cried	31
'Tis my happiness below	128
To Jesus, our exalted Lord	47
To Our Redeemer's glorious name	52
Triumphant Sion! lift thy head	147
Watchman! tell us of the night	16

INDEX OF HYMNS.

	HYMN
Welcome, sweet day of rest	94
When all thy mercies, O my God	77
When gathering clouds around I view	220
When I can read my title clear	112
When I survey the wondrous cross	25
When, Lord, to this our western land	153
When, marshal'd on the nightly plain	17
When this passing world is done	217
When through the torn sail the wild tempest	132
While shepherds watched their flocks by night	8
While Thee I seek, protecting Power	86
While with ceaseless course the sun	101
Who is this that comes from Edom	27
Who place on Sion's God their trust	126
With joy shall I behold the day	118
With one consent let all the earth	93
Ye boundless realms of joy	82
Ye faithful souls who Jesus know	34

INDEX OF PSALMS IN METER.

As pants the hart for cooling streams.......... 188
God, my King, thy might confessing......... 71
God's perfect law converts the soul............ 108
Have mercy, Lord, on me....................... 190
He's blest whose sins have pardon gain'd..... 172
In mercy, not in wrath......................... 166
In thee I put my steadfast trust............... 131
Jehovah reigns, let all the earth.............. 65
Lord, for ever at thy side...................... 125
Magnify Jehovah's Name....................... 63
No change of time shall ever shock........... 122
O bless the Lord, my soul...................... 83
O come, loud anthems let us sing............. 68
O God of hosts, the mighty Lord............. 96
O Lord, thy mercy, my sure hope. 197
O render thanks and bless the Lord........... 170
O render thanks to God above................ 61
O 'twas a joyful sound to hear................ 150
The Lord himself, the mighty Lord.......... 196
The Lord, the only God, is great............. 149
Through all the changing scenes of life...... 81
Thy chastening wrath, O Lord, restrain...... 178
Thy presence, Lord, hath me supplied........ 123
Who place on Sion's God their trust. 126
With one consent let all the earth.... 93
Ye boundless realms of joy.................... 82